NCTE's Theory and Research into Practice (TRIP) series presents volumes of works designed to offer a teacher audience a solid theoretical foundation in a given subject area within English language arts, exposure to the pertinent research in that area, and a number of practice-oriented models designed to stimulate theory-based application in the reader's own classroom.

Volumes Currently Available in the Series

Writing about Literature
2nd ed., Revised and Updated

Larry R. Johannessen
Northern Illinois University

Elizabeth A. Kahn
James B. Conant High School
Hoffman Estates, Illinois

Carolyn Calhoun Walter
University of Chicago Laboratory Schools

National Council of Teachers of English
1111 W. Kenyon Road, Urbana, Illinois 61801-1096

Staff Editor: Carol Roehm-Stogsdill

Interior Design: Doug Burnett

Cover Design: Jody A. Boles

Cover Image: iStockphoto.com/Amanda Rohde

NCTE Stock Number: 32111

It is the policy of NCTE in its journals and other publications to provide a forum for the open discussion of ideas concerning the content and the teaching of English and the language arts. Publicity accorded to any particular point of view does not imply endorsement by the Executive Committee, the Board of Directors, or the membership at large, except in announcements of policy, where such endorsement is clearly specified.

Every effort has been made to provide current URLs and email addresses, but because of the rapidly changing nature of the Web, some sites and addresses may no longer be accessible.

Library of Congress Cataloging-in-Publication Data

Johannessen, Larry R.
     Writing about literature / Larry R. Johannessen, Elizabeth Kahn, Carolyn Calhoun Walter. — 2nd ed., rev. and updated.
          p. cm. — (Theory and research into practice (TRIP) series)
     "NCTE Stock Number: 32111."
     Includes bibliographical references.
     ISBN 978-0-8141-3211-1 ((pbk))
  1. English language—Composition and exercises—Study and teaching (Secondary)
I. Kahn, Elizabeth A.   II. Walter, Carolyn Calhoun.   III. Title.
     LB1631.J63 2009
     428.0071'2—dc22

                                                          2008053881

This book is dedicated to our students who continue to remind us what we too often take for granted; that is, that interpreting and writing about literature are extremely complex and must be taught in ways that will engage students in the essential skills and strategies.

Contents

Contents

Foreword

Michael W. Smith
Temple University

When Jeff Wilhelm and I talk about our study of the literate lives of young men both in and out of school (Smith & Wilhelm 2002, 2006), we're often asked about whether the young men in our study spoke of a preference for their male English teachers over their female English teachers. Our answer often surprises. None of the young men whom we interviewed made any kind of distinction between their men and women teachers. But many of them made another kind of distinction about their teachers, identifying two groups of teachers about whom they felt very differently: the helpers and the assigners. Here's Wolf, a twelfth grader articulating a common complaint:

> I mean you are a teacher I assume that you teach, I am going to assume . . . obviously you have some amount of homework that, there is going to be some amount of homework involved in teaching no matter what happens. That is a given, but my teachers will just give out thousands and thousands [of] pages of homework and expect that to teach you. They don't teach. It is just like do chapters, questions 1–5. And then they are going to assume that you know it because you do the questions 1–5 and even if you talk with somebody, you aren't going to know it. But if you actually get up there and teach it to people and ask questions they are going to know it. That is why America is stupid.

Wolf explains that assigning isn't the same as teaching. It seems obvious, but I'm afraid it isn't, especially when it comes to the teaching of writing. In my experience, by far the dominant mode of instruction is what I call the assign-and-assess approach. That is, teachers assign writing and then grade it, using their comments both as a way to justify the grade and as a way to provide instruction for future work. This model is especially common when teachers ask students to write about literature, the presumption being that if students understand the literature they've read, they'll be able to write about it.

Common though it may be, the assign-and-assess model of teaching doesn't work for students or for teachers. It doesn't work for students because it presumes that they learn best from their mistakes. But what Jeff and I found is that the single factor that most motivates students' engagement is a sense of competence. That is, students (like all of us, we would argue) like to do what they're good at and avoid doing what they don't feel good at.

The model also doesn't work for teachers. Let's do a thought experiment: What part of your job do you least enjoy? My bet: responding to students' papers. But the assign-and-assess mode of teaching requires hours and hours spent responding to students' work because response is the primary (or even sole) method of instruction. There has to be a better way.

In *Writing about Literature, 2nd ed., Revised and Updated* three remarkable teachers show readers a better way. Drawing on compelling research and theory, Larry Johannessen, Elizabeth Kahn, and Carolyn Calhoun Walter explain and then enact a model for instruction that has proven to be far, far more effective than assign-and-assess. They carefully articulate what it takes to write effective arguments about literature. They provide wonderfully engaging activities to help students develop such crucial skills as distinguishing evidence from claims, generating convincing evidence, and developing clear explanations of the significance of evidence. They share their recognition that effective writing requires deep and active reading and present sequences of activities to foster that kind of reading. The activities they share are sure to help students gain rich insights into the characters that populate the stories and poems they read and the ideas that inform those texts.

The activities promise more than just helping students become better readers and writers, as crucially important as those skills are. They promise to transform classrooms into sites of collaborative inquiry and engaged conversation, where students and teachers work together to grapple with the issues that make our profession so fulfilling. They promise to make teaching an act of preparing students to be successful rather than remediating them after they have failed.

When Larry, Betsy, and Carolyn told me that an elaborated and updated version of *Writing about Literature* was on the way, I couldn't have been more delighted. Over the years I have leant my old copy out more than any other book I own. For good reason. The book is smart, knowing, and humane. Larry, Betsy, and Carolyn understand literature, writing, and kids. I've used ideas and activities I learned from reading it in teaching in middle schools and high schools and in my work with preservice and inservice teachers.

You're in for a treat.

References

Smith, M. W., & Wilhelm, J. (2002). *"Reading don't fix no Chevys": Literacy in the lives of young men*. Portsmouth, NH: Heinemann.

Smith, M. W., & Wilhelm, J. (2006). *Going with the flow: How to engage boys (and girls) in their literacy learning*. Portsmouth, NH: Heinemann.

Acknowledgments

First, we acknowledge our indebtedness to George Hillocks Jr., who is a major influence on our thinking about interpreting and writing about literature. Many years ago, George, more than anyone else, shaped our thinking about how to design thoughtful, engaging instruction to teach students to make inferences about literature and turn their interpretations into compositions. Furthermore, he helped us to understand the critical role of student interaction and authentic discussion in these complex processes.

We are also indebted to our many friends and acquaintances from our days at the University of Chicago who have had a significant impact on our thinking about teaching. The Chicago group is much too large to list here, but Tom McCann, Peter Smagorinsky, Michael Smith, Joseph Flanagan, and Steve Gevinson have been our close friends and collaborators for a number of years and deserve special recognition.

In addition, we want to thank Kurt Austin, who has been a wonderful editor and who encouraged, prodded, and supported us throughout the process. Staff Editor Carol Roehm-Stogsdill provided attention to detail and steady leadership in guiding the project into print.

We acknowledge a special debt to our many students. From our work with them, we have learned much about interpreting and writing about literature. We also want to thank the many colleagues we have worked with over the years who have helped shape our views of teaching.

1 Theory and Research

The 2004 "NCTE Beliefs about the Teaching of Writing" articulates a plethora of purposes that result in writing: "Purposes for writing include developing social networks; engaging in civil discourse; supporting personal and spiritual growth; reflecting on experience; communicating professionally and academically; building relationships with others, including friends, family, and like-minded individuals; and engaging in aesthetic experiences" (p. 4).

Certainly, all of these purposes merit our students' attention, practice, and development within the English writing curriculum. Our intent is to focus upon students' development of writing skills related to "engaging in civil discourse" and "communicating professionally and academically." In *Clueless in Academe*, Gerald Graff (2003) makes the case that these two purposes in fact overlap, forming a "culture of ideas and arguments":

> By the culture of ideas and arguments, I refer to that admittedly blurry entity that spans the academic and intellectual worlds on the one hand and the arena of journalistic public discourse on the other.... What these different types [academics and professionals] have in common, from the research professor to the newspaper editorialist to the mythical educated lay person on the street, is a commitment to articulating ideas in public. Whatever the differences between their specialized jargons, they have all learned to play the following game: listen closely to others, summarize them in a recognizable way, and make your own relevant argument. This argument literacy, the ability to listen, summarize, and respond, is rightly viewed as central to being educated. (pp. 2–3)

Writing in the Classroom

As part of the English curriculum, our students engage in the study of literary texts. Real issues and real differences of opinion arise from the study of these texts. When students write about their ideas, explaining and supporting them while taking into account the ideas of others, they are using the medium of argument. In doing so, they are practicing the metacognitive skills that will stand them in good stead as both professionals and informed citizens. As Graff (2003) suggests, "The point is not to turn students into clones of professors but to give them access to forms of intellectual capital that have a lot of power in the world" (p. 9).

The formal argument provides the ideal venue for students to articulate their ideas about literature. As a student of ours once remarked, "I now see that I can have any idea I want to have about the literature. I just have to have the evidence to prove it!" And, we would add, "the explanations" as well. Explanations are, in fact, where students use the text at hand to explain and prove their insights about it.

What one reader sees within a piece of textual evidence may or may not be readily discernable to another reader. In a conversation, listeners may ask for clarification of points or signal their confusion visually, prompting the speaker to elaborate further upon a point being made. Such clues are not available to solitary writers. They cannot assume that their readers automatically "see what they see." According to Shaughnessy (1977), students used to conversational turns tend to assume that "the reader understands what is going on in the writer's mind and needs therefore no introductions or transitions or explanations" (p. 240). Thus, Graff (2003) argues the need for specific instruction in "elaborated code" (p. 58), or, in other words, in getting students to provide the contexts and explanations that are so vital to a fully developed argument.

Student Response to Literature and Writing Achievement

In 2005 the National Assessment of Educational Progress reported the results (NCES 2005) for 9-, 13-, and 17-year-olds' achievement in reading during the last three decades. The report indicates that in 2004 most 13-year-olds and 17-year-olds had "partially developed skills and understanding associated with reading" (p. 3). Reading performance involving "understanding complicated information," such as interpreting a challenging literary text, was demonstrated by only 38 percent of 17-year-olds (p. 3).

These results clearly indicate the need for effective instruction that will help students move beyond decoding and literal level understanding of texts. According to at least one national report, the National Commission on Writing in America's Schools and Colleges (2003), writing should be the centerpiece of a good education because "writing is how students connect the dots in their knowledge" (p. 3).

Writing beyond the Classroom

Writing as a workplace skill seems more important than ever. The National Commission on Writing in America's Schools and Colleges (2003) asserts, "Although only a few hundred thousand adults earn their living as full-time writers, many working Americans would not be able to hold their positions if they were not excellent writers" (p. 10). Further underscoring its point, the Commission also cites Richard Light's (2001) workplace statistic: "More than 90 percent of midcareer professionals recently cited the 'need to write effectively' a skill 'of great importance' in their day-to-day work" (p. 11).

Argument literacy is not only "central to being educated" (Graff 2003, p. 3) but also "central to getting things done" in the "real" world beyond the schoolroom. When a research scientist writes a grant proposal, he must take into account what others have done in the field and what others may be proposing to do and then explain how his approach is different from and better than those of others in order to obtain funding. When a lawyer presents her closing arguments, she may well summarize/acknowledge her opponent's case before going on to summarize her own, reviewing her own conclusions and explaining why her facts and evidence outweigh those of the opposition. When an ad executive "pitches" his new campaign to a client, he presents his ideas and explains the merits of his approach and why it is better than those of the competition.

We are not suggesting a direct leap from students' writing about literature to preparing a legal brief. In our previous hypothetical examples, there is much content-specific knowledge. In a recent review of research on writing in the professions, Anne Beaufort (2006) acknowledges that "No amount of preparation in school can equip one fully for content-specific writing tasks in professional life" (p. 229). Yet her review of relevant research over the past twenty years does suggest some ways in which transfer from classroom to workplace is possible and useful in terms of social and metacognitive processes. Beaufort cites Dias, Freedman, Medway, and Pare's study (1999) of four school/workplace contexts for writing. Their research suggests that writing for thinking and oral social skills were two skills that did transfer (p. 231). Beaufort (2006) also cites her own work (1998, 1999) involving an ethnographic study of four successful writers working within a nonprofit agency. Beaufort found that among other skills, "critical thinking skill fostered by academic writing tasks" provided writers with a useful base for "adding context-specific knowledge" (p. 231).

Beaufort (2006) further summarizes her 1999 study's findings regarding workplace communication by detailing several areas of necessary and overlapping knowledge: "discourse community knowledge, subject matter knowledge, genre knowledge, rhetorical knowledge, and writing process knowledge" (p. 234). Classroom writing can certainly give students knowledge of the final three. And while classroom writing cannot substantively provide the first two types of knowledge, it can give students practice in answering real questions and collecting and assessing data, skills that should aid in acquiring and using discourse community knowledge and subject matter knowledge. Beaufort's review suggests that workplace writers have a sense of "writing as a problem-solving process" (p. 220) as do students who ask and answer genuine questions about their texts. Furthermore, in their study of writing in the workplace, Sellen and Harper (2002) note that in the workplace it is "the process of taking notes that is important in helping [workers] to construct and organize their thoughts" (p. 63). It is not information per se that gives these workers skill but rather the interaction with and assessment of that data. To take effective notes, these workers must ask questions regarding their data: What is most important? What is most relevant? What will I need to further my case, to solve the problem at hand? In the "information age," the skills necessary to assess information will stand our students in good stead.

What Is Basic to Interpreting Literature?

In reflecting on how to engage students in interpreting literature and defending their ideas in writing, we must first ask: What is involved in understanding literature? Logic tells us that students' writing about a literary work will not be very meaningful if they do not understand the work they are trying to write about. What does a reader have to know or be able to do in order to understand a literary work?

Textbooks, handbooks, and curriculum guides often suggest that understanding literature involves understanding a number of literary terms. The ninth-grade textbook *Holt Elements of Literature. Third Course* (Beers & Odell, 2005) presents a list of eighty-five terms in the "Handbook of Literary Terms" in the back of the anthology. The list includes terms such as *alliteration, allusion, blank verse, character, connotation/denotation, dramatic monologue, figure of speech, foreshadowing, imagery, irony, plot, point of view, satire, setting, symbol,* and so on. The eleventh-grade text (Beers & Odell, 2005) contains one hundred-fifty-four terms, and another ninth-grade text, *Prentice Hall Literature: Timeless Voices, Timeless Themes. Gold Level* (2000), presents one hundred-fifteen terms. When faced with such extensive lists, teachers may find it difficult to know where to begin.

Many of the terms are somewhat problematic. For example, *Prentice Hall Literature: Timeless Voices, Timeless Themes* defines *theme* as "a central message or insight into life revealed through the literary work" (2000, p. 1011). This text presents a thematic unit in which all of the works involve

"Visions of the Future." If a student were asked the theme of Isaac Asimov's short story "The Machine That Won the War," one of the selections in the thematic unit, would "Asimov believes that people will rely on computers in the future" or "The author believes that in the future there is life beyond Earth" be satisfactory responses? According to the teacher's notes in the text, both of these responses are acceptable answers and interpretations of the theme of the story. However, these responses do not reflect a very sophisticated interpretation of Asimov's "theme." Does identifying Asimov's vision that people will rely on computers in the future as a "theme" reflect the same skills as explaining the author's generalization that heavy reliance on computers is dangerous and might lead to some negative consequences?

In addition, are the skills involved in determining the theme of a fable when a moral is explicitly stated at the end the same as those involved in determining the theme of a work when it is implied and never directly stated? Do these extensive lists of terms represent basic skills involved in interpreting literature? Are skills taxonomically related; in other words, are there some skills that must be mastered before others can be learned?

Recognizing the importance of questions like these in arriving at a framework for instruction in literature, many theorists, researchers, and textbook editors have attempted to define the skills basic to the comprehension of literature and have hypothesized various skill hierarchies. Yet most of these hypotheses have not been substantiated by empirical testing. Hillocks and Ludlow (1984) present a taxonomy that is strongly supported by empirical evidence. It is also highly effective as a foundation for designing instruction for helping students learn to interpret literature.

The Hillocks and Ludlow Taxonomy of Skills in Reading and Interpreting Fiction

Hillocks and Ludlow's (1984) skill levels are clearly defined, and there is strong evidence of their hierarchical and taxonomical relationship. In co-research with Bernard McCabe and James E. McCampbell (1971) and independently (1980), Hillocks identifies seven skill types and corresponding question types. Following is his explanation of the seven levels from simplest to most complex. The skill types are not meant to be exhaustive but represent key skills that Hillocks indicates are of apparent concern to reading teachers, teachers of literature, and literary critics. They correspond to the skills the NAEP report (NCES 2005) identifies as important in raising student achievement.

The first three skill types are literal level skills. They require identification of information that appears explicitly in the text. The next four skill types are inferential level skills that require generalizations about the relationships that are not stated in the text. The questions illustrating each of the skill levels are based on Chapter 1 of *The Pearl* (1972) by John Steinbeck. These questions comprise one of the four question sets examined in Hillocks and Ludlow's study.

Literal Level of Comprehension

1. Basic Stated Information—Identifying frequently stated information that presents some condition crucial to the story.
Example: What happened to Coyotito?

2. Key Detail—Identifying a detail that appears at some key juncture of the plot and bears a causal relationship to what happens.
Example: Where did Coyotito sleep?

3. Stated Relationship—Identifying a statement that explains the relationship between at least two pieces of information in the text.
Example: What was the beggars' reason for following Kino and Juana to the doctor's house?

Inferential Level of Comprehension

4. Simple Implied Relationship—Inferring the relationship between two pieces of information usually closely juxtaposed in the text.
Example: What were Kino's feelings about the pearls he offers the doctor? Explain how you know.

5. Complex Implied Relationship—Inferring the relationship(s) among many pieces of information spread throughout large parts of the text. A question of this type might concern, for example, the causes of character change. This would involve relating details of personality before and after a change and inferring the causes of the change from the same details and intervening events.
Example: In this chapter, Kino appears at home and in town. He feels and acts differently in these two places. Part of the difference is the result of what happened to Coyotito. Part is the result of other things. (a) What are the differences between the way Kino acts and feels at home and in town? (b) Apart from what happened to Coyotito, explain the causes of those differences.

6. Author's generalization—Inferring a generalization about the world outside of the work from the fabric of the work as a whole. These ques-

tions demand a statement of what the work suggests about human nature or the human condition as it exists outside the text.
Example: What comment or generalization does the chapter make on the way "civilization" influences human behavior and attitudes? Give evidence from the story to support your answer.

7. Structural Generalization—Generalizing about how parts of the work operate together to achieve certain effects. To belong properly to this category, a question must first require the reader to generalize about the arrangement of certain parts of a work. Second, it must require an explanation of how those parts work in achieving certain effects.
Example: Steinbeck presents a group of beggars in the story. (a) Explain what purposes they serve in relationship to the first eleven paragraphs of the story. (b) Present evidence from the story to support your answer.

In designing questions for these skill types, it is important to note that a question must be classified as a skill type in conjunction with the text from which it is derived. For example, if *The Pearl* contained explicit statements telling how and why Kino acted differently at home and in town, question five could not be classified as a complex implied relationship question. For the same reason, for a fable with an explicitly stated moral, a question that asks what the fable shows about human nature could not be considered an author's generalization question if a literal statement of the moral provides a satisfactory answer to the question.

The Hillocks and Ludlow Study

In Hillocks and Ludlow's study, sets of questions, including the one previously cited, for four different stories were administered to students from ninth grade to graduate school. The number of students responding to each question set ranged from seventy-seven to one-hundred-twenty-seven. Student scores were analyzed to determine hierarchical and taxonomical relationships of items on the individual tests using a form of the Rasch psychometric model known as the ordered categories model (Wright & Masters, 1982; Wright, Masters, & Ludlow, 1981), which considers partial and full credit. The results of the statistical analysis strongly support the hypotheses of the study: that the items are hierarchical and taxonomically related to each other. In other words, the question types are arranged from easiest to most complex, and the question types are taxonomical—readers will tend not to be able to answer question seven if they could not answer question six, or not be able to answer questions five, six, or seven if they could not answer question four, and so forth.

Some Implications of the Hillocks Taxonomy

Hillocks's taxonomy helps us not only to identify some of the complex skills involved in interpreting fiction but also to design instruction to help students master these skills. The results of Hillocks and Ludlow's study indicate the need to work hierarchically in helping students understand literature at higher levels. The teacher can use the question types to construct inventories (diagnostic tests or tools) to evaluate the skills of individual students and classes. For example, a teacher might have students read Chapter 1 of Steinbeck's *The Pearl* (or one of the short stories Hillocks and Ludlow use in their study) and answer the questions Hillocks and Ludlow developed for each of the question types. Or she might use the taxonomy to develop a set of questions for a chapter from another novel or short story. After evaluating students' responses to the questions and determining at what level students can work comfortably in interpreting literature in general, she can design instruction to guide her students in dealing with the next higher levels.

Working hierarchically is necessary. For example, if we want students to understand the author's generalizations in a given work, we need to be sure that they first understand the lower level relationships (Hillocks & Ludlow, 1984). But Hillocks warns that working at two or more levels above student competence is likely to result in failure to comprehend, frustration, and hostility toward literature. Although this taxonomy admittedly does not include all possible types of questions, it provides a basis for gauging what level of skill is required by specific questions and composition assignments. Also, it provides a framework for developing discussion questions and composition assignments appropriate for the level of a particular class.

Using the Taxonomy as a Framework for Instruction

Some authorities are wary of questioning hierarchies. For example, Christenbury and Kelly (1983) are wary of questioning hierarchies because of the way "many questioning schemata have been abused and have become prescriptions rather than suggestions or guidelines" (p. 5). Alexander, Jetton, Kulikowich, and Woehler (1994) warn that any taxonomy can be misleading and even dangerous. They maintain that teachers think they must always ask one question from each category and that teachers often ask unrelated questions without considering that the questions should point to important and related content. These are, of course, important caveats. Working with a hierarchy should not be done in an inflexible way that suppresses responses that do not follow a prescribed pattern.

Even though some have expressed concerns about using taxonomies, McCann, Johannessen, Kahn, and Flanagan (2006) note that several taxonomies have influenced educators in expressing instructional goals and have aided teachers in developing questions to focus reading and to prompt discussion. They present and discuss taxonomies developed by Bloom (1956) and Pearson and Johnson (1978), as well as Hillocks. McCann et al. (2006, p. 103) then examine important similarities (see Figure 1.1).

The three taxonomies, Pearson and Johnson (1978), Bloom (1956), and Hillocks and Ludlow (1984), are similar in that all three share levels that seem to correlate to three levels of comprehension: literal or explicit information, textually implicit information, and scriptally implicit information or generalizations from the text to the world beyond the text. As McCann et al. (2006) point out, "No matter how one conceives of the levels of difficulty in comprehension and different levels of question types, it is important for teachers to recognize that the different levels exist" (p. 102). This has important implications for planning instruction designed to help students learn to interpret and write about literature.

The Hillocks Taxonomy and Vygotsky

Assessing students' levels of competence on the reading hierarchy and then designing activities and questions that will enable them to reach the next higher levels is consistent with Russian psychologist Lev Vygotsky's zone of proximal development (ZPD). Vygotsky (1978) defines his concept as the distance between a child's "actual developmental level as determined by independent problem solving" and his or her higher level of "potential development as determined through problem solving under adult guidance or in collaboration with more capable peers" (p. 86). Although Vygotsky's ideas originally were developed with respect to instruction leading to psychological development, many others (e.g., Bruner, 1962; Wells, 2000; Smagorinsky & Fry, 1993; Hedegaard, 2005) have seen the implications and applications for pedagogic theory and practice. In fact, in his review of research regarding middle and high school composition from 1984–2003, Hillocks (2006) notes a decided shift from educational researchers' reliance on the developmental theories of Piaget in the 1960s and 1970s to those of Vygotsky in the final decades of the century. Hillocks states that "Vygotsky (1978) makes a strong case that 'learning results in mental development' and makes development possible (p. 90)" (p. 49). Noting this, Hillocks identifies the teacher's task as "not one of waiting for the learner to develop and for learning to appear

HILLOCKS AND LUDLOW (1984)	BLOOM (1956)	PEARSON AND JOHNSON (1978)
Basic Stated Information: Identifying frequently stated information that represents some condition crucial to the story.	**Knowledge:** Bringing to mind specifics, methods, patterns, structures, or settings.	**Textually Explicit:** Dealing with obvious answers that are "right there in the text."
Key Detail: Identifying a detail that appears at some key juncture of the plot and that bears a causal relationship to what happens in a narrative.		
Stated Relationship: Identifying a statement that explains the relationship between at least two pieces of information in the text.	**Comprehension:** Summarizing, paraphrasing, interpreting facts, as opposed to just recalling them.	
Simple Implied Relationship: Inferring the relationship between two pieces of information usually closely juxtaposed in the text.	**Application:** Using abstractions (such as rules of procedure, generalized ideas, or methods) in particular and concrete situations.	**Textually Implicit:** Dealing with a level of comprehension in that there is at least one step of logical or pragmatic inferring necessary to get from the question to the response and both the question and the response are derived from the text.
Complex Implied Relationship: Inferring the relationship among many pieces of information spread throughout large parts of the text.	**Analysis:** Clarifying the basis for an arrangement of a communication.	
Author's Generalization: Inferring a generalization about the world outside the work from the fabric of the work as a whole.	**Synthesis:** Putting together, arranging and combining pieces of data in such a way as to have a structure or pattern not clearly there before.	**"Scriptally" Implicit** Dealing with a level of comprehension in which the data base for the inference is in the reader's mind, not just on the page.
Structural Generalization: Generalizing about how parts of the work operate together to achieve certain effects.	**Evaluation:** Judging the value of materials and methods for a given purpose or purposes.	

Figure 1.1. Three Taxonomies

naturally, but of finding ways to promote learning in the zone of what the student is capable of doing with help so that development takes place" (p. 49).

Among the pedagogic ideas drawn from Vygotsky's research is instructional scaffolding. In his introduction to *Introduction to Vygotsky*, Harry Daniels (2005) cites Vygotsky within his explanation of scaffolding: "The scaffolding interpretation is one in which a distinction is made between support for the initial performance of tasks and subsequent performance without assistance: 'the distance between problem-solving abilities exhibited by a learner working alone and that learner's problem-solving abilities when assisted by or collaborating with more-experienced people' (Vygotsky, 1978, p. 86)" (p. 6). If the goal of reading and literary instruction is to develop students' abilities to comprehend increasingly complex and sophisticated texts independently, then Hillocks's reading hierarchy provides a framework for both assessing students' current abilities and designing instruction that will enable them to move forward at a challenging yet appropriate level.

Writing to Express Interpretations

Although Hillocks's question sets were not used to evaluate writing *per se*, the questions at levels five, six, and seven are typical of composition assignments often given to students. Questions at these levels are complex enough to generate lengthy compositions. In Hillocks and Ludlow's (1984) study, good answers for, say, a complex implied relationship question usually ranged from two to five sentences. The following is an answer to the question about how and why Kino acts and feels differently at home and in town. In the study this answer was rated as "good." (Answers were rated either "wrong," "partly right," or "good.")

> At home Kino feels comfortable, secure, and peaceful (that is until the scorpion stings Coyotito). In town he is nervous and afraid. The difference is caused by the bad way the townspeople have treated his race. They treat his race like animals. He is afraid of their power over his people but also angry that they have this power.

What is needed to expand this kind of response into an effective essay? Toulmin's (1958) and Toulmin, Rieke, and Janik's (1984) analyses of argument help answer this question. A response to a complex implied relationship, author's generalization, or structural generalization question is an argument in the sense that the writer is attempting to convince a reader that his conclusions about the text are accurate. Toulmin identifies three basic parts of an effective argument—claim, data, and warrant.

The *claim* is the conclusion (or generalization) that is advanced; the *data* are the evidence or the specific details presented in support of the conclusion; and the *warrant* is the explanation of why the data justify the claim or, in other words, authorization for the "leap" from the data to the claim.

An analysis of the previous answer in Toulmin's terms reveals that it is basically a series of claims that could be elaborated with data and warrant(s). An effective composition on this question would perhaps begin with the ideas presented in the previous answer as a series of claims to be argued (the "thesis"), and the body of the composition would present evidence and warrants for each of the claims. For the first claim, for instance, "At home Kino feels comfortable, secure, and peaceful," evidence might include quotations from the novel such as, "Kino heard the little splash of morning waves on the beach. It was very good—Kino closed his eyes again to listen to his music" (pp. 1–2). At another point, the novel states that as Juana ate her breakfast, "Kino sighed with satisfaction" (p. 4). The music or family song Kino hears at home is described as "an aching chord that caught the throat, saying this is safety, this is warmth, this is the *Whole*" (p. 3).

This kind of analysis reveals some skills in addition to those suggested by the taxonomy that students need in order to write effective essays interpreting complex implied relationships, author's generalizations, and structural generalizations. They must identify their claims, find supporting evidence for each, organize their evidence, smoothly incorporate evidence in their papers, and explain how their evidence justifies the claims. As the National Commission on Writing in American Schools and Colleges (2003), NAEP (NCES 2005), and our experience in the classroom suggest, students have difficulty with these skills. Furthermore, being able to answer successfully a level five, six, or seven question in a short paragraph, such as the one previously for *The Pearl*, does not automatically mean that the student can write an effective argument on the question. Students may be able to make insightful claims but not be able to support those claims in a composition.

Often we have found that students use virtually no data at all, presenting claim after claim without any support. This makes a very weak composition even though some of the claims may be insightful. We've also found that sometimes our students state a claim (x), then present an extended summary of what happens in a story or novel, and conclude with the idea "all of this shows x." In this case they lose the focus of their argument with considerable irrelevant detail. This seems to be what many teachers are frustrated about when they say that their students' writing is "plot summary" rather than "analysis." Students developing their papers in this manner need to learn how to select and use appropriate evidence.

One of the greatest difficulties, even for competent writers, is providing warrants. How many times have we all heard our students tell us something such as, "But the evidence speaks for itself"? They assume that the leap from data to claim is obvious and that it is, therefore, not necessary to elaborate on the connection between the two. In some cases the relationship may be fairly obvious, but most often it is not. For example, a student writer might use as evidence of Kino's fear in town the fact that he removes his hat when he knocks at the door of the doctor's house. Without a warrant explaining why the writer concludes that removing his hat shows fear, the reader may not be convinced by this evidence. He may conclude the action shows respect or good upbringing instead of fear.

The difference between a good answer to a complex implied relationship question and a good composition of literary analysis suggests that whereas reading and writing may be "reflections of the same cognitive process" (Squire, 1983, p. 582), they also require a shift in focus for the student. Reading and responding to literature require students to focus on a topic (What do they know?), but writing a persuasive composition requires students to focus on a goal (What do they want to do with what they know?). In Squire's terms, the learner is *reconstructing* the structure and meaning of another writer in comprehending; whereas the learner is *constructing* meaning and developing ideas in composing. Flower and Hayes seem to agree with this concept of construction. As they note, "In composing, writers often work from the bottom of a tree [hierarchy] to more inclusive steps" (1977, p. 460). However, Flower and Hayes (1977) identify a problem at this point, "But, readers [of analytic prose] understand best when they have an overview, when they can see an idea structure from the top down" (p. 460). It is not enough then for the writer to *know* something from reading. The effective writer is aware of this shift in focus from what she knows to what she does with what she knows. She is aware of this difference between the manner in which she privately constructs a conclusion and the manner in which it is best presented to a reader who has not been privy to her thought processes. How can we design instruction to provide students with the kind of argument literacy they need to write compositions that are clear and convincing for readers?

What Works in Teaching Writing

What methods and approaches are most effective in helping middle and high school students learn to write well? Langer (2001) examines three groups of teachers in urban schools with diverse populations, some of which consistently beat the odds by helping students to higher achievement in English than socioeconomic data would predict. Langer (2001) finds that "all of the more successful teachers overtly taught their students strategies for organizing their thoughts and completing their tasks, whereas only 17 percent of the more typical teachers did so. The other 83 percent of the more typical teachers left such strategies implicit." For example, Langer (2001) indicates that "Most teachers in the higher performing schools share and discuss with students rubrics for evaluating performance; they also incorporate them into their ongoing instructional activities as a way to help their students develop an understanding of the components that contribute to a higher score" (p. 868). The higher-performing schools emphasized teaching procedures or metacognitive knowledge. However, Langer (2001) adds that "in more typical schools, instruction focused on the content or the skills, but not necessarily on providing students with procedural or metacognitive strategies" (p. 869).

Langer (2001) also finds that high-performing teachers create interactive, social contexts for learning. In schools that beat the odds,

> English learning and high literacy (the content as well as the skills) were treated as social activity, with depth and complexity of understanding and proficiency with conventions growing out of the shared cognition that emerges from interaction with present and imagined others. [The more typical classrooms] emphasized individual activity and individual thinking, with students tending to work alone or to interact primarily with the teacher. Even when group work occurred in such classrooms, the activity usually involved answering questions rather than engaging in substantive discussion from multiple perspectives. (p. 872)

Applebee, Langer, Nystrand, and Gamoran (2003) and Nystrand (2006) report that a growing body of research reveals that discussion-based instruction, in the context of high academic demands, significantly enhances literacy achievement. Engagement in authentic or dialogic discussion—as opposed to recitation—resulted in enhanced reading comprehension and literacy skills. Fisher (2006) and Fisher and Frey (2003) found that instruction is most effective when it progresses from teacher-led modeling of procedures and strategies to small-group collaboration in which students practice the procedures and strategies to independent work in which students apply the procedures and strategies individually on their own. Fisher argues that the most important—and most often neglected—part of this instructional process is the small-group collaboration in which students work together without the direct guidance of the teacher.

Hillocks (1986, 2006) reports that results of a meta-analysis of various approaches to teaching writing reveal that by far the most effective approaches "had clear objectives and emphasized strong interaction among students and the teacher about the focus of instruction" (2006, p. 70). The most effective instruction focused on teaching "task-specific procedural knowledge" and "inquiry, learning strategies for producing the content of specific writing tasks" (p. 70). The focus on inquiry was much more effective than focusing instruction on the study of models.

Furthermore, Hillocks found that focusing on task-specific procedural knowledge and inquiry is more effective than teaching what has been called "the writing process." A focus on the writing process generally involves students in learning techniques such as brainstorming, freewriting, mapping, and so forth to generate ideas for writing. Students frequently engage in peer response activities and in revising, editing, and publishing their writing. However, these general skills may not help students learn and practice the specific procedural knowledge involved in writing a literary analysis. As Smagorinsky and Smith (1992) explain, while some authorities claim that general knowledge is sufficient to guide all writing, others maintain that "the complexity and demands of particular tasks require more specialized knowledge" (p. 287). They go on to explain that because the knowledge that students must learn is "task-specific," the instruction needs to be "differentiated" and is "dependent on the particular demands of individual tasks" (1992, p. 288). Finally, Smagorinsky and Smith (1992) point out, "Pedagogy based on the assumption that composing knowledge is task-specific requires an analysis of the particular knowledge required for each type of composition and explicit instruction in the appropriate set of procedures" (p. 288).

In summary, approaches that are most effective focus on teaching students task-specific procedural knowledge and inquiry through scaffolding instruction so that students practice targeted strategies by engaging in activities that involve high levels of student collaboration and gradually increase the level of student independence. As Smith and Wilhelm (2006) explain, designing instruction that focuses on procedural knowledge and inquiry requires the following:

1. Identifying the knowledge experienced writers employ to write a particular kind of text, focusing especially on procedural knowledge;

2. Helping students develop the knowledge they need by providing plenty of practice, focusing especially on meaningful social activity;

3. Moving students to independent application of the knowledge. (p. 128)

Research Using the Toulmin Model

Research involving instruction using the Toulmin model of argument suggests its efficacy for writing instruction and improving writing. In his review of middle and high school composition research from 1984–2003, Hillocks (2006) reports on a study by McCann (1989) using the Toulmin model of argument to examine sixth-, ninth-, and twelfth-grade students' knowledge of and ability to make arguments in writing. In analyzing students' writing in response to a prompt regarding whether students could leave school for lunch, McCann found that students at all grade levels included claims (reasons for support of the proposition) but that "at all grade levels students had difficulty incorporating data or evidence into their texts" (Hillocks, 2006, p. 71). McCann also asked students to read and rank constructed passages of argument ranging from "carefully developed passages with all parts of an argument to a passage with only a narrative" (Hillocks, 2006, p. 71). Students at all three grade levels "rank ordered the three most complete arguments as did the expert adults, indicating that they are able to recognize [effective] arguments" (Hillocks, 2006, p. 71).

These findings suggest that writing effective arguments is within students' zone of proximal development and that teaching students to identify, assess, and incorporate data into their arguments would be useful instructional steps. The significant results of two other studies (Connor, 1990; and Yeh, 1998) highlighted by Hillocks (2006) provide further strong support for using the Toulmin model for instructional purposes: it helps teachers identify and focus instruction on the procedural knowledge involved in developing an argument.

Formulas for Writing

Some teachers and researchers have argued that instruction focusing on teaching formulas, such as the five-paragraph theme, tends to result in shallow, formulaic writing (Hillocks, 2002). So wouldn't this problem also result from focusing on the Toulmin template of claim, data, and warrant? One of our sophomore students once remarked about his confidence in going ahead with an English assignment, "English papers I understand: you've got your claim. Then, you've got your context, evidence, explanation; context, evidence, explanation."

There are differences, however, between the five-paragraph formula and Toulmin. The Toulmin model prompts students to develop certain kinds of content for their writing. For example, it prompts them to find evidence to support a claim and to identify the warrant that links the evidence to the claim. It prompts them to identify alternative explanations or opposing arguments and to address them. In contrast, the five-paragraph format, as Hillocks (2002) explains, typically asks students to state an opinion and then to "suggest reasons why they think their opinion is justified. These reasons are to be developed by adding other relevant sentences, but not necessarily evidence to support the asserted reasons" (p. 201).

In justifying the formats for argument that he gives his students, Gerald Graff (2003) asserts, "all communication is partly formulaic. Formulas can enable creativity and communication as often as they can stifle them. If we refuse to provide such formulas on the grounds that they are too prescriptive or that everything has to come from the students themselves, we just end up hiding the tools of success" (p. 11).

We use the Toulmin model to identify procedures that students need to learn in order to develop effective arguments and, in this case, effective arguments about literature. In other words, it helps us in doing a task analysis. The practice section includes instructional activities that are scaffolded to enable students to learn these procedures or strategies for generating arguments rather than merely to imitate a formula.

Why Task Analysis Is Important

As Smagorinsky and Smith (1992) indicate, each writing task involves task-specific knowledge, and if teachers want their students to learn the skills and subskills involved in writing an effective literary analysis, they will need to do a careful analysis, task analysis, of the skills and subskills involved in such tasks in order to plan effective instruction.

Literature texts provide a wide scope of readings, literary terms, and writing assignments. This scope allows teachers to select materials that are interesting to and appropriate for their students. In providing this breadth, however, textbooks, by their very nature, cannot provide the necessary depth required to set up effective writing about literature. Take, for example, a writing assignment presented after students read "The Cask of Amontillado" by Edgar Allan Poe in the *Holt Elements of Literature. Third Course* (Beers & Odell, 2005, p. 181). Students are asked to assume that Montresor is arrested and that they are to write a speech for either the prosecution or the defense arguing that Montresor is either insane (defense attorney) or that he knew exactly what he was doing and planned the murder in advance (prosecutor). On the surface, this assignment has several advantages that make it attractive: a sense of "real world" application, a defined audience, and a clear point to argue. Teachers selecting this writing prompt might well assume that students would find this role-play engaging and fun.

Yet a closer look at the assignment suggests that students would need several important subskills and additional information in order to complete it successfully. To ensure that students move beyond such undeveloped and idiosyncratic definitions as the following, students would need much clearer definitions of the target terms used for either thesis.

> Montresor is insane because he murdered Fortunato. Murder is not a rational act.

> Montresor murdered Fortunato to avenge a perceived "insult." In this case, the punishment does not fit the crime, so Montresor is insane.

A legal insanity defense is based upon an absence of willful intent and awareness: the defendant "at the time of the commission of the acts constituting the offense" due to "severe mental disease or defect" was "unable to appreciate the nature and quality of the wrongfulness of his acts" (Insanity defense, 2006, 'Lectric Law Library online). Establishing insanity also rests upon two distinguishing criteria in this case: an inability to distinguish fantasy from reality and uncontrollable impulsive behavior. Thus, a student taking the defense attorney position would have three possible claims to prove: (1) Montresor was unable to distinguish whether his actions were right or wrong at the time of his crime. (2) Montresor was unable to distinguish fantasy from reality at the time of his crime. (3) Montresor's behavior at the time of his crime was uncontrolled and impulsive.

Conversely, the prosecuting attorney would need to prove: (1) Montresor was aware that his actions were wrong at the time of his crime. (2) Montresor was able to distinguish fantasy from reality at the time of his crime. (3) Montresor's actions demonstrate planning and intent. To be effective, each of these claims would need supporting evidence [direct quotes] from the text and explanations showing how the evidence supports the claim. At the very highest level of response, the prosecution or defense also would take into account the arguments of the opposition. In fact, a close reading of "The Cask of Amontillado" suggests that a defense of insanity would be very hard to mount. Thus, there is little or no controversy inherent within this assignment.

Looking more fully at what students are being asked to do in "The Cask of Amontillado" assignment, teachers may wish to give students additional information (for example, the criteria for establishing insanity), to modify the assignment (perhaps asking students to take the role of the prosecuting attorney but to identify and refute possible evidence for the defense), or to have students work on specific aspects of the assignment (for example, an activity in which students identify which criterion for sanity Montresor's "putting on a mask of black silk" [p. 175] supports and explain how this textual evidence proves it).

Teachers want to read good papers and want students to succeed in assigned tasks. In order to do this, we need more than engaging assignments. We need to analyze the final product that we are asking students to produce in order to identify the information and skills they need to execute it successfully. Such task analysis lies at the center of purposeful rhetorical instruction. Furthermore, teachers need to assess which of these skills students already have and which they need to practice in order to complete the writing assignment successfully. Once again, we need to be aware of our students' zones of proximal development.

Such a task analysis approach is consistent with Wiggins and McTighe's (1998) concept of backward design. Wiggins and McTighe identify three stages in their backward design process: (1) identify the desired results [students' independent demonstration of acquired skills/ knowledge]; (2) determine acceptable evidence [task analysis: determine what skills and information students need to complete the assignment successfully]; and (3) plan learning experiences and instruction [assess students' current competencies and design activities and instruction to give students expertise in new areas].

Principles of Sequencing and Activity Design

In designing the instruction in the Practice section, we used the following principles of sequencing and activity design derived from the theory and research findings previously presented.

1. The activities move from the kinds of interpretations with which students are more comfortable (making simple inferences) to those that are more difficult or challenging for them (interpreting complex implied relationships and author's generalizations).

2. The activities focus on helping students learn procedural knowledge

that will enable them to turn their understanding of literature into what some call analytic, persuasive writing and others call argument. Students practice stating a position or viewpoint, collecting evidence to support their position, evaluating their evidence, and articulating the relationship between their evidence and their claims. They learn to anticipate objections to their interpretations and respond to the objections.

3. The activity sequences involve high levels of collaboration and student interaction, moving from teacher-led discussion to small group collaboration to independent work.

4. The activity sequences provide scaffolding for students so that they have more support from the teacher and from teacher-designed materials in the early stages of learning a procedure. The activities and sequences gradually reduce the amount of support and become more open-ended.

5. The activities are designed to capture student interest and engagement—to pose interpretive problems that will be intriguing to students. Introductory activities are close to student experiences and are designed to elicit students' opinions and prior knowledge and to "hook" students on some of the key concepts on which the literature will focus.

6. The activities focus on knowledge of form when students have developed the procedural knowledge necessary to generate substance or content.

   The activities explained in the Practice section are intended to serve as a model for activity design and sequencing that teachers can follow in creating materials to meet the needs and interests of their own students. We present the activities as they would be used with specific literary works in order to illustrate the procedures and classroom dynamics. We have chosen literary works and authors that are widely used in secondary-level English curricula and that represent various genres, cultures, and levels of sophistication. The sequences are designed to help students interpret literature at higher levels and write effective compositions expressing their interpretations. We are not, however, suggesting that the activities we present comprise a complete instructional unit for the literature included. We would expect them to be part of the instruction (such as study guides, vocabulary activities, media presentations, role-playing, oral presentations, productions, projects, and so forth) designed to guide students in understanding each work as a whole.

2 Practice

Supporting an Interpretation Sequence

Typically, we have found that students at the secondary level tend to include many claims in their writing without providing specific supporting evidence to back them up. Or, they sometimes tend to support a claim with a lengthy retelling of the story, neglecting to explain any connection between the events they describe and their claims. Much of the time they seem to argue with "blinders on," not recognizing or responding to counterarguments and counterevidence that readers will likely raise. However, there is a solution. When we engage our students in activities that help them learn to interpret simple and complex implied relationships in a novel and that also help them develop the skills Toulmin (1958) identifies as basic to argument—finding evidence (data) to support a claim and linking the evidence and the claim with warrants—they become more effective writers. In addition, we have discovered that having our students work on anticipating and responding to counterarguments and counterevidence increases the sophistication of their arguments.

The activities in this sequence, designed to help students interpret simple and complex implied relationships and practice the skills Toulmin (1958) identifies as basic to argument, have been designed for *To Kill a Mockingbird* (1960) by Harper Lee and *The House on Mango Street* (1989) by Sandra Cisneros but could be easily adapted to work well with other literary works that raise questions about whether a specific character is a good female role model or whether the work as a whole presents good female role models. The sequence of activities is designed to prepare students to write a persuasive composition arguing whether a work includes or lacks good female role models or whether a specific character is a good female role model.

We are not suggesting that these are the only activities a teacher would include in a unit featuring either of these novels or any novel. They are intended to be included along with other activities designed to help students engage in studying the literary work.

Discussing Scenarios: What Makes a Good Female Role Model?

This activity involves students in thinking about what makes a good female role model and is designed to pique their interest in this concept. It introduces them to strategies basic to argument—elaborating their reasoning for an audience, providing evidence, and defending their views when challenged. It prepares them for later activities in which they argue an interpretation about literary characters. Specifically, it prepares them for analyzing literary characters in order to determine whether they are characterized as good female role models.

In this first activity of the sequence, students individually examine short scenarios describing eight females (see Handout 2.1, p. 31). For each scenario, they decide whether the person is a good female role model and explain why or why not. After students have thought about their own views, we ask them to work in small groups of three or four. Each group tries to reach a consensus about each of the eight scenarios and then lists the characteristics of a good female role model that have emerged from their discussion. After the small group work, students report their ideas in a whole-class discussion.

Scenarios work best when they are created to stimulate debate. The situations in this set of scenarios are arguable rather than clear cut. For example, some of our students argue that Lucy Lee is a good role model because she is able to overcome obstacles in her life. But others are quick to respond that because she made serious mistakes in her life, such as dropping out of school and having a child at age 15, she is not a good role model. One of our students countered this point by stating, "Everyone makes mistakes so if that's your definition, then no one will ever be a role model." Still another student responded, "These are not little mistakes everyone makes, like getting a bad grade on a test; they're big mistakes that most people don't make." This discussion leads students to questions such as whether a person who makes serious mistakes can be a good role model and if so, under what conditions.

In addition, the situations in some of the scenarios are designed to be similar to characters or events in the novels. For example, Mary Hunter is a little like Miss Maudie, and Theresa Carrarra echoes some of the ideas expressed by Sandra Cisneros.

Because the scenarios lead to differing viewpoints, students challenge each other's views in the small-group and whole-class discussions. As they are challenged, they elaborate on their reasoning, provide specific supporting evidence, and respond to arguments made against them. Classroom discussions of the scenarios often become quite animated, with many students highly invested in the process and eager to express their views. We have found that even our "quiet classes" tend to have a lot to say.

During the whole-class discussion, it is helpful if the teacher or a designated student lists the characteristics of a good female role model that emerge from the discussion on the board or projects them so the class can record them for future use. One of our ninth-grade "regular level" classes created the following list: sticking up for what you believe in, putting your family first before yourself, doing what's right, and overcoming hardships or mistakes.

In this activity students can hardly avoid arguing a viewpoint and trying to persuade others by explaining their reasons and challenging the reasons or logic of others. In addition, if an activity such as this is done before students begin reading a novel such as *To Kill a Mockingbird* or *The House on Mango Street*, it leads to more purposeful reading. Students have something to look for as they read—to what extent the female characters (and, in comparison, the male characters as well) are good role models.

Brainstorming

This activity focuses on having students think about arguments that can be made on both sides of the following issue.

For *To Kill a Mockingbird*: Some readers have criticized Harper Lee's *To Kill a Mockingbird* for not presenting good female role models. They argue the novel has strong male role models, including Atticus Finch, Tom Robinson, Jem Finch, and Sheriff Tate, but that it is lacking in good female role models. Others argue there are good female role models among the female characters, such as Miss Maudie, Calpurnia, Aunt Alexandra, Mrs. Dubose, and even Scout. Does *To Kill a Mockingbird* lack good female role models?

For *The House on Mango Street*: Some readers have criticized Sandra Cisneros's *The House on Mango Street* for not presenting good female role models. At one point, Esperanza says that Mexicans "don't like their women strong" (p. 10). On the other hand, others have argued that there are good female role models in the novel, such as Alicia, Esperanza, and Esperanza's mother. Does *The House on Mango Street* lack good female role models?

Handouts 2.2 and 2.3 on pp. 33–34 present a chart that students can use to record their ideas. Examples are provided with the charts to help students understand the kinds of things that should be included and to push them to return to the text for specific details and evidence. Students work in small groups of three or four to generate as many ideas as they can. Small groups then report their findings in a whole-class discussion. During the class discussion, it is useful to have a student list ideas on the board or use whatever technological device may be available to project ideas for the class to see. Often in small groups, if everyone in the group initially tends to be on one side of the issue, students may have difficulty anticipating what the other side may argue. The whole-class discussion tends to bring out additional views and helps students to see arguments of the other side. It usually takes some practice with several activities in this sequence for students to develop the insight to anticipate arguments of their opposition.

Overall, the brainstorming activity helps students examine the issue from both sides before making up their minds about their own viewpoint. It helps them begin to learn an effective strategy—thinking of arguments and evidence on each (or all) sides of an issue—that they can use in approaching any composition involving argument and persuasion. A key to the success of a brainstorming activity like this is that it involves a genuinely arguable issue with legitimate supporting evidence for both sides.

A variation of this activity is to involve students in blogging as an alternative to an oral class discussion. Setting up a classroom blog using a website such as blogger.com works well. We either give students a few days to post entries and read and respond to their classmates' posts, or we have students blog for a class period in a computer lab.

As students first begin blogging, we have found that they each tend to state their own viewpoint and do not respond to the views of others. For example, a student will write an entry such as the following: "I think Aunt Alexandra is a good role model because she tries to help out by being like a mother to Jem and Scout." Another student will write, "I don't think Mrs. Dubose is a good role model because she yells mean things at Jem and Scout." At first students will rarely respond to others' posts. One way we've encouraged students to respond to each other's ideas is to jump in ourselves and model this kind of response. We've added a comment to the blog such as the following: "Matt, you make a good point about Mrs. Dubose being really mean, but Atticus calls her courageous and a great lady. He seems to think she's a good role model. Why does he say this? Do you agree or disagree with his thinking?" Or we might comment, "Lashey, can you think of any examples of how Aunt Alexandra acts like a good mother to Jem and/or Scout?" By starting the process of responding to specific points and encouraging students to do the same, we have found that students begin to pick up the idea themselves.

Once students have blogged on the issue, we compile (cut and paste) some of the key ideas that emerged and bring them into class for further discussion.

One caveat we would add is that when using a blog as a classroom activity, we have found that it is important to set some ground rules, such as using standard spelling and mechanical conventions and using respectful, school-appropriate language, etc. Since blogger.com is on the Internet, we ask students to use only their first name as their posted name (no last names and no made-up names), and we set up the blog to allow comments only by those that the administrator of the site (the teacher) invites to join the blog (the students in the classroom).

Claim or Evidence?

Most middle and high school students have difficulty distinguishing between claims and evidence. When asked to support their views, they often provide a series of claims without providing specific supporting evidence. For example, our students might typically write:

> Aunt Alexandra is a poor role model. She is racist and tends to judge people based on their appearance. This does not show Jem and Scout the right way to live their lives.

Or for *The House on Mango Street*, they might write:

> Sally is not a good role model because she got married before eighth grade and lets her husband push her around all the time.

Students tend not to realize that the statements "she is racist," "she tends to judge people based on their appearance," and "she lets her husband push her around all the time" are claims or generalizations that need to be supported with specific evidence. They omit possible evidence such as Scout's statement that "let a sixteen-year-old girl giggle in the choir and Aunty would say, 'It just goes to show you, all the Penfield women are flighty'" (Lee, 1960, p. 129), or the narrator's explanation that Sally's husband "won't let her talk on the telephone. And he doesn't let her look out the window. And he doesn't like her friends, so nobody gets to visit her unless he is working" (Cisneros, 1989, pp. 101–02).

The activity "Claim or Evidence?" is designed to help students understand what is involved in providing specific evidence for claims. Students are given the activity sheet "Claim or Evidence?" for one of the novels (see Handouts 2.4 and 2.5 on pp. 35–36). The sheet provides five short paragraphs for them to analyze. For each paragraph, they determine what claim is made; whether the claim is a valid, justifiable claim; whether there is specific evidence provided in the paragraph to support the claim; and what specific evidence or additional evidence, if any, from the novel could be included to support the claim.

Students work on this activity in small groups of three or four. This format allows students to discuss and refine their initial responses. Students who are less certain about what constitutes good evidence can receive help and guidance from other students who have a better understanding of the concept. After small groups have completed their work, it is beneficial to assign each group a different paragraph and ask them to present their findings to the whole class.

An effective follow-up assignment asks students to choose one of the paragraphs that they have determined lacks effective supporting evidence and revise it so that they remedy the problems.

Warrant Workout

Once students have worked on the difference between a claim and evidence, they will be ready to engage in writing warrants. We have explained to students that a warrant is the "link between the evidence and the claim" or "the explanation of how the evidence leads to the claim." For example, if a writer argues that Mrs. Dubose is a good female role model because she overcomes her addiction to morphine and provides evidence of her success and of the difficulty involved in this accomplishment, then the warrant is something like the following: someone who is strong and persistent enough to accomplish a difficult and painful goal is a good role model. The warrant is the guideline used to link the claim (Mrs. Dubose is a good role model) and the evidence (that she overcomes addiction to morphine). We don't necessarily always use the term *warrant* with our students because it is sometimes confusing to them or difficult for them to remember. As an alternative, we sometimes use *explanation* rather than *warrant* because in a sense the warrant is an explanation of how the evidence supports the claim.

Providing students with an example of claims, evidence, and warrants helps them to understand these abstract concepts. In this activity, students are given examples using the format of a chart, Handouts 2.6 and 2.7 (pp. 37–38). After students examine the examples provided on the chart, they then choose another claim or another piece of evidence that proves their position on the issue under consideration (whether *To Kill a Mockingbird* or *The House on Mango Street* presents good female role models). They add another claim, evidence, and warrant on the chart. Students can work on this activity in small groups or individually. When students have completed their work, it is effective to have some of them present their claim, evidence, and warrant to the whole class. If students work in small groups, each group can be given a large piece of butcher paper to write on so that their work can be posted on the walls of the classroom for everyone to see and discuss.

One problem our students tend to have when they include evidence in the form of direct quotations from the text is giving the reader enough information about the context of the quotation. For example, they will use a quotation such as Atticus's statement that Mrs. Dubose "was the bravest person I ever knew" (p. 112) without letting readers know when Atticus said this or what led him to say this about her. The examples provided on the chart can be used to have students examine ways they as writers can provide context for the direct quotations without retelling too much of the story. As students view or listen to their peers' claims, evidence (with context), and warrants, they should be encouraged to identify strengths and any aspects that may need to be clarified or better explained and so forth.

Responding to Counterarguments

We have found that the quality and depth of a student's composition is greatly increased when the writer anticipates and addresses counterarguments and/or counterevidence—whether directly or indirectly. Engaging students in anticipating and responding to counterarguments helps them internalize this important process and makes it more likely that their arguments will be more thoughtful and convincing.

Again, using a chart form (see Handouts 2.8 and 2.9, pp. 39–40), we add an example of a counterargument and response to the claim, evidence, and warrants that students examined in the previous activity. Working in small groups or individually, students are then asked to return to the claim, evidence, and warrant that they created in the previous activity and now add a counterargument and response.

Using an issue such as the one we have used in this sequence (whether *To Kill a Mockingbird* or *The House on Mango Street* lacks good female role models)—about which students have differing viewpoints—helps them learn how to anticipate and respond to counterarguments and counterevidence. Also they understand the need to do so as they are directly challenged by other students who do not agree with their position.

When our students first begin trying to incorporate counterarguments within their writing, they often struggle with how to do so. Some will simply start a paragraph asserting an opposite viewpoint to their position, rather than introducing the counterargument with a phrase such as, "Some people argue that . . . " or "Those who argue that Calpurnia is not a good role model say that. . . . " For example, if they are arguing that Calpurnia is a good role model, they may begin a later paragraph by stating, "Calpurnia is not a good role model because she doesn't voice her views about Tom Robinson's case." Of course, when counterarguments are raised without any identification, the writing is very confusing because the writer appears to switch to arguing an opposite viewpoint. It is important to brainstorm with students various ways that they can introduce a counterargument and ways they can smoothly transition to a response to that counterargument, such as "The problem with this argument is . . . " or "Although it may be true that Esperanza is sometimes weak, in this case. . . . "

We have found that simplifying Toulmin's model (Toulmin, 1958; Toulmin, Rieke, & Janik, 1984), as we have done in this sequence, makes it accessible for middle and high school students. While some teachers have questioned whether the Toulmin model promotes formulaic writing, as does the often maligned model of the five-paragraph theme, we have found that the Toulmin model differs from the formula for the five-paragraph theme because it helps students to generate rich, thoughtful content for their writing. The formula of the five-paragraph essay does not specifically identify what information students need to generate and, therefore, often leads to shallow "blether" (Hillocks, 2002, p. 122). As Gerald Graff (2003) suggests, it is not the idea of a formula that is the problem but rather whether the formula is effective in helping students become better communicators. We have found that using the Toulmin model truly helps our students write more effective arguments.

Organizing for Writing

At this point in the sequence, students are usually ready to write a composition arguing their viewpoint on the issue of whether the novel studied—either *To Kill a Mockingbird* or *The House on Mango Street*—presents good female role models. An alternative is to have students write a composition arguing whether a certain character in either novel is or is not a good female role model, a character such as Esperanza in *The House on Mango Street*, or Aunt Alexandra, Calpurnia, Mrs. Dubose, or Scout in *To Kill a Mockingbird*.

We provide students with a graphic organizer to help them plan their writing. We create a chart similar to the ones that are provided in this sequence with boxes for claims, evidence, warrants, counterarguments, and response to counterarguments. Another approach that is quite effective is to have students use a software program, such as "Inspiration," that enables them to create their own graphic representation to help them plan their composition. For example, they may state a claim in a circle with boxes branching from the circle, each containing a piece of supporting evidence. Then, branching from each piece of evidence, they might have an oval with the warrant written inside and so on. With this software, students can also use different shapes or colors to identify claims, evidence, and warrants.

Before students begin drafting a composition, it is helpful to have them examine a written argument such as the excerpt in Handout 2.10 from a student composition arguing whether Aunt Alexandra is a good role model. The "Questions for Analysis" help students evaluate the strengths and weaknesses of the writing. Students discuss the excerpt from the composition and the questions in small groups of three to four. Each group is asked to present their responses to some of the questions in a whole-class discussion. This activity works best if the teacher selects a composition with some strengths but also some weaknesses. Then students have a number of issues that they can talk about. For example, the student composition on page 41 (see Handout 2.10) contains an effective specific quotation that provides evidence of Aunt Alexandra's stereotyping of poor families in Maycomb. On the other hand, it lacks specific evidence to prove the point that Aunt Alexandra thinks it was right for Tom Robinson to die. In addition, while the composition makes some good points, it also has some awkwardly worded sentences and a sentence fragment. (Of course, if a piece of writing from a student in the class or another class is used, then the student's name should not be identified.) After students have seen and evaluated an example of a written argument, they are ready to draft their own.

Peer Response

When students have completed drafts, they are ready to work in teams to examine their own writing to identify strengths and some ways to improve their arguments. We divide the class into groups of three and give each group a set of colored highlighters. The students focus on one composition at a time, reading it together. They highlight the writer's overall position on the issue in one color. They use another color to highlight claims, another color for evidence, and another color for warrants. This process helps students identify whether they are missing any of these important elements of an argument.

The next step involves looking at each of the compositions to answer the following questions: (1) What opposing arguments or counterarguments has the writer anticipated? (2) How does the writer respond to or address each of the counterarguments? Students are encouraged to identify the strengths of each composition and make suggestions to help the writer in revising.

If students have access to a computer lab and have their compositions on flash drives, they can do the procedures described previously on the computer, using the highlighting tool and the insert comment tool.

Using the feedback from their peers, students then revise their work. Students may enjoy posting their final compositions in the classroom so they can compare their own views to those of others.

Handout 2.1. What Makes a Good Female Role Model?

<u>Directions</u>: Read each of the following scenarios. For each scenario, decide whether the person is or is not a good female role model. Also explain the reasons for your viewpoint. After considering the scenarios and the reasons for your viewpoint on each, make a list of what you believe are the characteristics of a good female role model.

Nicole Lewinski is a kicker on the boys' varsity football team at her high school. Many students and adults at the school think she was crazy to try out. They urged her to be content playing on the girls' soccer team. Nicole says she has always loved football, and the only way she can play competitively is to be on the boys' football team.

Sally Hightower has been a lawyer for ten years. When she has twins, her husband, who is also a lawyer, begs her to give up her career to stay home and raise the twins. She is hesitant to give up her law career that has always been her dream and that she finds very fulfilling but decides that she will give it up if her husband feels so strongly about her staying home with their children.

Tanesha Brown believes in what she calls "old-fashioned values." She believes that the man is the head of the family and that women should not work outside the home; women should stay home, raise their children, cook, and clean. She believes that men are more suited to the working world and women to the hearth and home. She tries to instill these values in her children.

Mary Hunter lived some years ago when women were not permitted to serve on juries and most were discouraged from attending college or having careers. She opposed these practices, as well as laws that would not allow African Americans to have the same rights that whites had. Even if many of her friends and acquaintances disagreed, she expressed her views when she felt it was appropriate to do so, but she was always careful not to be too aggressive in expressing her opinions.

Toni Maloney did not like school. She was frequently absent and rarely did any schoolwork, so she failed many courses in high school. She is very attractive, and at age 17, she was able to obtain a modeling job, which eventually leads to her having a successful career as a "super model" by the age of 20.

Lucy Lee had a tough life. She dropped out of school at age 15 when she had her first child. At age 17, she was a single mother with three children and no support from the father. She received welfare in order to survive. At age 20, with the help of her mother who watched her children, she was able to go back to school at night. She received her GED and was accepted at a local college. At 26, she graduated with a college degree in accounting and was able to get a good job that enables her to have her own house and provide for her children.

Theresa Carrarra is an internationally acclaimed writer. She is unmarried and has no children. In her books and speaking engagements, she tells women in her audiences who are single and do not have children that they should be grateful and proud of being unmarried and without children because they have independence that women who are married and/or mothers do not have.

Nina Pinta is a person who says what she thinks and has few, if any, friends. Some people say that she is mean and insulting; others describe her as blunt and outspoken. She has little patience with people whom she believes are lazy or unmotivated and she tells them exactly what she thinks of them. She was born with a partially paralyzed leg but participated in grueling workouts every day, eventually gaining a spot on the Olympic track team. She never was able to achieve a medal in the Olympics, but her doctors said they were amazed that she was able to accomplish what she did.

List the characteristics of a good female role model.

Writing about Literature, 2nd ed., Revised and Updated by Larry Johannessen, Elizabeth A. Kahn, and Carolyn Calhoun Walter © 2009 NCTE.

Handout 2.2. Brainstorming: Female Role Models in *To Kill a Mockingbird*

Some readers have criticized Harper Lee's *To Kill a Mockingbird* for not presenting good female role models. They argue that the novel has strong male role models, including Atticus Finch, Tom Robinson, Jem Finch, and Sheriff Tate, but that it is lacking in good female role models. Others argue that there are good female role models among the female characters, such as Miss Maudie, Calpurnia, Aunt Alexandra, Mrs. Dubose, or even Scout. Does *To Kill a Mockingbird* lack good female role models? What arguments do you think readers might raise on each side of this issue? On the following chart, list additional arguments and evidence for each side of this issue.

It lacks good female role models.	*It includes good female role models.*
Example: At the missionary circle meeting, when Scout is asked whether she wants to be a lawyer when she grows up, she replies, "Nome, just a lady." Scout thinks about being a nurse or an aviator, but in the end doesn't stand up for herself and just tells the ladies what they want to hear.	*Example:* At the potential lynching of Tom Robinson, Scout stands up to the crowd and her actions save Atticus and Tom Robinson.

Writing about Literature, 2nd ed., Revised and Updated by Larry Johannessen, Elizabeth A. Kahn, and Carolyn Calhoun Walter © 2009 NCTE.

Handout 2.3. Brainstorming: Female Role Models in *The House on Mango Street*

Some readers have criticized Sandra Cisneros's *The House on Mango Street* for not presenting good female role models. At one point, Esperanza says that Mexicans "don't like their women strong" (10). Others have argued that there are good female role models in the novel, such as Alicia, Esperanza, and Esperanza's mother. Does *The House on Mango Street* lack good female role models? What arguments do you think readers might raise on each side of this issue? On the following chart, list additional arguments and evidence for each side of the issue.

It lacks good female role models.	It includes good female role models.
Example: Rafaela, Mamacita, Sally, and Minerva are weak and powerless, stuck in abusive relationships. Sally, for example, was abused by her father and marries a marshmallow salesman who won't let her talk on the telephone, look out the window, visit with her friends, or go outside without his permission.	*Example:* Esperanza's mother advises her to be strong and independent. She tells Esperanza to go to school and study hard: "'Look at my comadres.' She means Izaura whose husband left and Yolanda whose husband is dead. 'Got to take care all your own,' she says shaking her head."

Writing about Literature, 2nd ed., Revised and Updated by Larry Johannessen, Elizabeth A. Kahn, and Carolyn Calhoun Walter © 2009 NCTE.

Handout 2.4. *To Kill a Mockingbird*: Claim or Evidence?

Answer the following questions for each brief paragraph that follows:

- What claim is made?
- Is the claim a valid, justifiable claim? Why or why not?
- Is specific evidence presented to support the claim? Explain.
- Is there evidence (or other evidence) in the novel to support the claim? Cite this evidence.

1. Miss Caroline is obviously not a good female role model. She is a terrible teacher. The first-grade class dislikes her and has no respect for her. She is scared and weak.

2. Females in the novel are considered inferior to males. Jem tells Scout she is "gettin' more like a girl every day" (p. 52) when she is worried about Jem and Dill's plan to peep in the Radley window.

3. Miss Stephanie Crawford is a stereotypical female who is obsessed with gossip. She is always spreading rumors and gossip about people in Maycomb. She has her nose in everyone else's business.

4. Scout is a better fighter than most boys her age. She beats up boys regularly and won't take anything from anyone.

5. Calpurnia is a good female role model because she learned how to read and write and taught her son Zeebo when there weren't any schools for African Americans in the South. She taught Zeebo to read from the only books she had, the Bible and Blackstone's *Commentaries*. Jem was "thunderstruck" that she "taught Zeebo outa *that*" (p. 125).

Writing about Literature, 2nd ed., Revised and Updated by Larry Johannessen, Elizabeth A. Kahn, and Carolyn Calhoun Walter © 2009 NCTE.

Handout 2.5. *The House on Mango Street*: Claim or Evidence?

Answer the following questions for each brief paragraph below:

- What claim is made?
- Is the claim a valid, justifiable claim? Why or why not?
- Is specific evidence presented to support the claim? Explain.
- Is there evidence (or other evidence) in the novel to support the claim? Cite this evidence.

1. Esperanza is weak because she is ashamed of where she lives and the kind of life she leads. She hates her house and the places where her family lives. She does not have pride in herself and her family.

2. Esperanza's mother is very smart, making her a good role model. *eh* Esperanza reveals that her mother can speak two languages, sing opera, and fix a TV. She "borrows opera records from the public library" (p. 90) and learns all the songs. Her mother explains that she "didn't have nice clothes," but she "had brains" (p. 91).

3. Esperanza's aunt finds Esperanza her first job at Peter Pan Photo Finishers. But when Esperanza starts the job, she is shy and afraid.

4. Esperanza is strong because she is determined to overcome the poverty and prejudice that surrounds her as a young girl. She has goals for her life and shows a great deal of determination to achieve her goals.

more specific evidence

5. Most of the women in the novel are victims of abusive relationships and are too weak to recognize their situation and overcome their problems. They are poor role models because they stay with men who continue to abuse and belittle them. Minerva is abused by her husband but keeps forgiving him: "Then he is sorry and she opens the door again" (p. 85).

Writing about Literature, 2nd ed., Revised and Updated by Larry Johannessen, Elizabeth A. Kahn, and Carolyn Calhoun Walter © 2009 NCTE.

Handout 2.6. Warrant Workout: *To Kill a Mockingbird*

Does *To Kill a Mockingbird* present good female role models?

YES	NO
CLAIM: Mrs. Dubose is a strong female role model because she is able to overcome her morphine addiction.	CLAIM: The adult women in the novel express the view that females should be polite and ladylike rather than strong, assertive, and independent.
EVIDENCE (with context): Atticus tells Jem and Scout that Mrs. Dubose was a morphine addict but that her doctor put her on the drug as a painkiller because she was very ill and in agony. Atticus says, "Mrs. Dubose won, all ninety-eight pounds of her. According to her views, she died beholden to nothing and nobody. She was the bravest person I ever knew" (p. 112).	EVIDENCE (with context): In her "campaign to teach [Scout] to be a lady," Aunt Alexandra had Scout wear "her pink Sunday dress, shoes, and a petticoat." Aunt Alexandra and Calpurnia showed Scout how to serve refreshments. Calpurnia tells Scout, "You be still as a mouse in that corner an' you can help me load up the trays when I come back" (p. 228).
WARRANT (Explanation): Mrs. Dubose was strong and courageous because she accomplished a difficult and physically painful goal. Atticus considers Mrs. Dubose braver than anyone else he knows.	WARRANT (Explanation): Aunt Alexandra and Calpurnia are not good female role models because they convey the view that women should be good hostesses and conform to their society's stereotypes of a lady—being concerned primarily about clothes, cooking, and entertaining, and being quiet and submissive.
CLAIM:	CLAIM:
EVIDENCE (with context):	EVIDENCE (with context):
WARRANT (Explanation):	WARRANT (Explanation):

Writing about Literature, 2nd ed., *Revised and Updated* by Larry Johannessen, Elizabeth A. Kahn, and Carolyn Calhoun Walter © 2009 NCTE.

Handout 2.7. Warrant Workout: *The House on Mango Street*

Does *The House on Mango Street* present good female role models?

YES	NO
CLAIM: Esperanza is a good role model because she has positive goals for her future.	CLAIM: Esperanza is childish and self-centered.
EVIDENCE (with context): In "Bums in the Attic," Esperanza says, "One day I'll own my own house, but I won't forget who I am or where I came from. Passing bums will ask, Can I come in? I'll offer them the attic, ask them to stay, because I know how it is to be without a house."	EVIDENCE (with context): She makes fun of her Aunt Lupe, who is dying. Esperanza and her friends play a game of imitating her sick and disabled aunt, even though her aunt was nice to Esperanza and praised her poem.
WARRANT (Explanation): Esperanza has goals for improving her life, but she also has compassion and concern for others who may not succeed.	WARRANT (Explanation): Esperanza did this without thinking about her aunt or her aunt's feelings; she only thinks of herself and her own amusement. She says that she doesn't know why they picked her aunt to make fun of, that maybe they were "bored" or "tired."
CLAIM:	CLAIM:
EVIDENCE (with context):	EVIDENCE (with context):
WARRANT (Explanation):	WARRANT (Explanation):

Writing about Literature, 2nd ed., Revised and Updated by Larry Johannessen, Elizabeth A. Kahn, and Carolyn Calhoun Walter © 2009 NCTE.

Handout 2.8. Responding to Counterarguments: *To Kill a Mockingbird*

Does *To Kill a Mockingbird* present good female role models?

YES	NO
CLAIM: Mrs. Dubose is a strong female role model because she is able to overcome her morphine addiction.	CLAIM: The adult women in the novel express the view that females should be polite and ladylike rather than strong, assertive, and independent.
EVIDENCE (with context): Atticus tells Jem and Scout that Mrs. Dubose was a morphine addict but that her doctor put her on the drug as a painkiller because she was very ill and in agony. Atticus says, "Mrs. Dubose won, all ninety-eight pounds of her. According to her views, she died beholden to nothing and nobody. She was the bravest person I ever knew" (p. 112).	EVIDENCE (with context): In her "campaign to teach [Scout] to be a lady," Aunt Alexandra had Scout wear "her pink Sunday dress, shoes, and a petticoat." Aunt Alexandra and Calpurnia showed Scout how to serve refreshments. Calpurnia tells Scout, "You be still as a mouse in that corner an' you can help me load up the trays when I come back" (p. 228).
WARRANT (Explanation): Mrs. Dubose was strong and courageous because she accomplished a difficult and physically painful goal. Atticus considers Mrs. Dubose braver than anyone else he knows.	WARRANT (Explanation): Aunt Alexandra and Calpurnia are not good female role models because they convey the view that women should be good hostesses and conform to their society's stereotypes of a lady—being concerned primarily about clothes, cooking, and entertaining, and being quiet and submissive.
COUNTERARGUMENT: <u>Some readers</u> may point out that Mrs. Dubose tells Jem and Scout, "Your father's no better than the niggers and trash he works for!" (p. 102). <u>Therefore</u>, how can anyone call her a role model?	COUNTERARGUMENT: Those who take a different viewpoint may argue that although Aunt Alexandra may not be the greatest role model, Calpurnia is not simply concerned with making Scout a quiet, submissive lady. She models strength by standing her ground when Lula criticized her for bringing Jem and Scout to her church.
RESPONSE: On the other hand, Atticus himself admits that she had "her own views about things, a lot different from mine." He still believes that she is a good role model of "what real courage is" (p. 112).	RESPONSE: On the other hand, everyone in Calpurnia's church disagrees with Lula and thinks she is a "troublemaker from way back" (p. 119), so it doesn't take a great deal of strength to oppose her; Calpurnia has a whole congregation backing her up.

Writing about Literature, 2nd ed., Revised and Updated by Larry Johannessen, Elizabeth A. Kahn, and Carolyn Calhoun Walter © 2009 NCTE.

Handout 2.9. Responding to Counterarguments: *The House on Mango Street*

Does *The House on Mango Street* present good female role models?

YES	NO
CLAIM: Esperanza is a good role model because she has positive goals for her future.	CLAIM: Esperanza is childish and self-centered.
EVIDENCE (with context): In "Bums in the Attic," Esperanza says, "One day I'll own my own house, but I won't forget who I am or where I came from. Passing bums will ask, Can I come in? I'll offer them the attic, ask them to stay, because I know how it is to be without a house" (p. 87).	EVIDENCE (with context): She makes fun of her Aunt Lupe, who is dying. Esperanza and her friends play a game of imitating her sick and disabled aunt even though her aunt was nice to Esperanza and praised her poem.
WARRANT (Explanation): Esperanza has goals for improving her life; she also has compassion and concern for others like her who may not succeed.	WARRANT (Explanation): Esperanza did this without thinking about her aunt or her aunt's feelings; she only thinks of herself and her own amusement. She says that she doesn't know why they picked her aunt to make fun of, that maybe they were "bored" or "tired."
COUNTERARGUMENT: Some readers will argue that Esperanza may have goals to improve her life, but she is not a good role model because she is ashamed of her life and her family. She explains, "I want a house on a hill like the ones with the gardens where Papa works. We go on Sundays, Papa's day off. I used to go. I don't anymore. . . . I don't tell them I am ashamed—all of us staring out the window like the hungry. I am tired of looking at what we can't have" (p. 86).	COUNTERARGUMENT: Others may argue that in the end, Esperanza is a good role model because she feels bad about making fun of her aunt. She realizes her mistake and is remorseful. She says, "We didn't know. She had been dying for such a long time we forgot" (p. 61).
RESPONSE: It is true that Esperanza is not perfect. She is only a teenager, and it's unrealistic to expect that she won't occasionally engage in some self-pity. This shows she is human. Ultimately her concern for bums shows that she is a good person underneath. Being perfect isn't a requirement for a role model or no one would be a role model.	RESPONSE: However, Esperanza herself says of her actions, "Most likely I will go to hell and most likely I deserve to be there" (p. 58). That shows she recognizes that she is not a good role model.

Writing about Literature, 2nd ed., Revised and Updated by Larry Johannessen, Elizabeth A. Kahn, and Carolyn Calhoun Walter © 2009 NCTE.

Handout 2.10. Excerpt from a Student Composition Arguing Whether Aunt Alexandra Is a Good Role Model

To Become a Good Role Model

Role models don't judge and discriminate against other people like Aunt Alexandra does. When Scout is talking about Walter Cunningham, her Aunt cuts in her conversation. She says "Don't be silly Jean Louise, the thing is, you can scrub Walter Cunningham till he shines, you can put him in shoes and a new suit, but he'll never be like Jem. Besides there's a drinking streak in that family a mile wide. Finch women aren't interested in that sort of people." Aunt Alexandra shows in what she said that she's discriminating against Walter's family. Also it shows her stereotyping the family and good role models don't act that way. In many ways she has shown that she's racist towards black people such as Tom Robinson and Calpurnia. When she said that Scout couldn't go to Cal's house and told Atticus to fire her. In her missionary circle, she believes that it was right for Tom Robinson to die when everyone knew he wasn't guilty.

In the outcome Aunt Alexandra didn't help Scout into being a lady, but it showed her how people really are. She's not a good role model for anyone. Scout's Aunt discriminates, stereotypes, and is racist. . . . Her Aunt didn't teach Scout to do anything, but show her how not to act and think of others.

—Kelly Anderson

Questions for Analysis

1. What claims does the writer make?

2. What evidence is provided to support the claims? How appropriate or effective is the evidence?

3. Does the writer include warrants to link the evidence and claim? Explain.

4. Does the writer anticipate possible counterarguments or counterevidence that could be raised against her arguments? Explain.

5. What are the strengths of the excerpt? What are the weaknesses? How would you improve it? Be specific.

Writing about Literature, 2nd ed., Revised and Updated by Larry Johannessen, Elizabeth A. Kahn, and Carolyn Calhoun Walter © 2009 NCTE.

Explicating Implied Relationships: Character Analysis

A typical assignment for secondary students asks them to write what is often referred to as a "character analysis." Such a task requires that students be able to interpret simple and complex implied relationships involving character. They must then translate their inferences into written products involving sophisticated arguments that take into account possible counterarguments and use specific textual evidence as support. The question is, how do we help students to accomplish this?

Smith (1991) points to research that suggests that making interpretive strategies the center of instruction teaches students something they can transfer to new situations and gives them more confidence in their responses to literature. He argues that through activities that engage students in practicing strategies in collaborative settings that gradually require greater independence, students acquire the procedural knowledge to make more sophisticated interpretations and write more sophisticated compositions.

We have found that focusing on teaching students how to analyze characters' values is an effective way to engage students in learning interpretive strategies, particularly interpreting simple and complex implied relationships. This engagement helps students learn the procedural knowledge needed to write a character analysis.

The first activity in the sequence, "What Are Your Values?" introduces a list of values that students will use later to analyze a literary character's values. Students analyze their own personal values as a first step in the sequence. The activity serves as a prereading activity to help students better understand the vocabulary that will enable them to talk about the values of a literary character. It also provides a means "into" the literature for students, fostering what Rosenblatt (1968) calls "fruitful . . . transactions between individual readers and individual literary works" (pp. 26–27) by beginning with students' assessments of their own priorities and motivating forces before asking them to identify the priorities and motivating forces of literary characters.

In the "Analyzing a Character" activity, students work with complex implied relationships and refine their argumentation skills. This activity as well as the ones that follow utilizes Alice Walker's short story "Everyday Use" (2007), an often-anthologized short story.

The activities, "Identifying Parallels: Collecting and Analyzing Evidence" and "Explaining Evidence: The Warrant Connection" provide students with opportunities to learn how to find and analyze evidence to support an interpretation and to explain how evidence supports their interpretation of change.

The "What If . . . ? Character Questionnaire" is designed to help students make initial inferences about a major character and practice skills essential to explicating inferences in written discourse. The activity models how to use character questionnaires with a major work commonly taught in the secondary English curriculum, Mark Twain's *The Adventures of Huckleberry Finn* (1965).

In the activity, "Character Values Composition," students are asked to pull together all that they have learned and practiced by writing an extended analysis of the changes in values of a major character. The activity models how to help students plan and write their compositions. Before students turn in their final compositions, they evaluate their peers' rough drafts as a final check, utilizing a rubric.

Several of the activities within this sequence contain either embedded or follow-up writing assignments that provide students with additional practice and serve as a means for checking on students' progress. Finally, it is important to note that while doing one or two of the activities outlined in the entire sequence might provide an interesting change of pace, this will probably not be enough for most students to master the interpretive strategies and writing skills described earlier (Johannessen, 2001; Johannessen, Kahn, & Walter, 1982).

What Are Your Values?

Before asking students to analyze a character in a work of literature, we begin by giving students a list of values and definitions (See Handout 2.11, Analyzing Values, p. 60) and asking them if any of the listed terms need further clarification. We find that providing students with lists of terms is a good way to stretch them and their ideas beyond a quick "first response." Rather than asking students to respond to an open-ended question such as "What do you value most?" presenting a list such as the one we provide gives them the opportunity to reflect upon more possibilities than the first one or two that leap into their minds.

Once students have reviewed the initial list, we pass out "What Are Your Values?" (Handout 2.12, p. 61) and ask them to follow the directions, ranking their own top four values with Number 1 being the greatest value, Number 2 the second most important, and so on. For the bottom values, students place their least important value in Number 22 at the bottom of the list, their second least important value above it in Number 21, and so on. Students also have the option of adding values to the list if they think of something that is not present. Usually students find that they value a number of items listed, and it becomes challenging for them to select the most important (or least important) and create a ranking.

Once students have completed a list of their own most important and least important values, we ask for their predictions about the values of the class as a whole by asking them to fill in the appropriate blanks on the handout. At this point we give students a 3 x 5 card and ask them to list their top four values and bottom four values in rank order as they are listed on their handout. We use these cards to tally the data for the class, but these data are not presented to the class until after a discussion of class predictions.

After collecting the cards, we lead a class discussion, asking students to explain their top and bottom values. This discussion is usually at a high level and interesting as students discuss the ethical and moral values that guide them as they live their lives. Also, we ask students to explain their predictions for the class as a whole and what leads them to make these predictions. Typically students will disagree. In one class, a group of students predicted that their classmates most value social acceptance and being liked by their peers. Others disagreed, responding that their classmates value friendship rather than social acceptance, that they care more about having a few good friends than about being popular with everyone.

After a discussion of the predictions, we reveal the actual compiled results (e.g., family was selected as Number 1 by 22 out of 30 students, etc.). Often students are surprised, for example, that more of their peers value education or family than they expected. They record the findings for the class on the handout and discuss possible reasons for any differences between their predictions and actual results.

A possible follow-up writing assignment asks students to state their top value and provide one or two specific examples of why they chose it or to identify one of their predictions that did not match the actual results for the class and explain how they might account for this discrepancy. This follow-up writing assignment challenges students to do some additional thinking about their values and gives them additional practice in stating and supporting a claim.

When we ask students to think about values in terms of their lives, we are asking them to do with their experience what we are going to ask them to do with literature: apply an interpretive strategy to their own experiences in the same manner that they will apply it to the experiences of a character in a work of literature.

Analyzing a Character

In the "Analyzing a Character" activity, students are given the same list of values (see Handout 2.11, p. 60) that they were given in the previous activity, but now they are asked to rank the most important and least important values for a character at the beginning and end of a story. Making the ranking requires students to interpret complex implied relationships from various pieces of information in the story. They must consider and weigh many different possibilities. In making their choices and later arguing them with peers in small-group and whole-class discussions, students practice supporting their claims with evidence from the story.

One work we often have used successfully is Alice Walker's "Everyday Use," (2007), a story of two rural Georgia women, Mama and her daughter Maggie, and a second daughter Dee, who has left them for college and city life but returns home for a visit ostensibly ready to embrace the rural heritage she previously had disdained now that it is in fashion.

Once students have read the story and have a basic understanding of it, we pass out the "Character Analysis" activity sheet (see Handout 2.13, p. 62) and the list of values titled "Analyzing Values" (see Handout 2.11, p. 60) if students do not already have it. Next, we ask students to rank the most important and least important values in order at the beginning and at the end of the story for the character Mama.

Giving students a specific task such as this, with many values from which to select, allows them to consider more options to an answer than they might consider on their own. If they are simply asked to identify a character's values without a list to examine, they usually struggle to identify any possibilities and rarely challenge anything that may be suggested. With something concrete in front of them from which to start, students become personally engaged in the question of what the character values and are less likely to accept an answer uncritically. Providing students with a list of values gives them a vocabulary to talk about a character's values and how and why those values have changed.

After students have completed their individual rankings, we put them in heterogeneous small groups of three to five students to compare their answers and attempt to reach a consensus on their rankings. Students soon realize that this is very challenging. Talking in their groups, students make some interesting discoveries about the character Mama.

As students discuss Mama's values, some students argue that she values appearance at the beginning of the story, citing evidence such as her dream in which she imagines she is "a hundred pounds lighter, my skin like an uncooked barley pancake" (p. 1091) or Mama's comment that "Dee is lighter than Maggie, with nicer hair and a fuller figure" (p. 1092). At the end of the story, they argue that she values fairness or equality and cite evidence such as Mama's giving the quilts that Dee wants to Maggie.

Another group of students may argue that Mama's most important value near the start of the story is respect from Dee, and they may cite early evidence such as Mama's saying, "I am the way my daughter would want me to be" (p. 1091). Still other students may claim that Mama is not motivated by fairness/equality at the end but rather by family. After all, they argue, Mama finally takes the quilts from Dee only after Maggie says that she can remember her dead grandmother without the aid of the quilts because, as Mama remembers, Grandma Dee had "taught her [Maggie] how to quilt herself" (p. 1097). Thus, Maggie has spent time with and been close to her family, and Mama wishes to acknowledge that. Students may also offer top values for Mama, such as peace or family at the beginning of the story, and power or peace at the end.

Most students soon discover that Mama is motivated by very different values at the beginning than she is at the end of the story. Students sometimes discover that the values they listed as most important for Mama at the beginning of the story are the ones they ranked as least important for her at the end of the story. Or they realize that a single value, such as peace, might be qualified or interpreted in one way at the beginning of the story and in a very different way at the end. Most significantly, when students discuss their rankings, they find specific and concrete ways to talk about the actions and motives of a literary character. As they debate possible values, they move beyond a literal understanding of the story and reach a fuller understanding of the character and what the author wants readers to understand about conflicting cultural values. In other words, they are interpreting simple and complex implied relationships among characters in the story. They are learning an important interpretative strategy.

Although it might seem that we are splitting hairs by asking students to reach a consensus in ranking a character's values within their small groups, we have found this directive useful in encouraging different responses and in promoting the kind of debate that calls for students to reexamine details in the text. The students must find evidence and explain what the evidence shows or means—something that we want them to do when they analyze a character orally or when we ask them to write about a character.

Once students in their small groups have reached a consensus on their rankings for Mama's values at the beginning and at the end of the story (or once they realize that they are unable to reach a consensus), we have them reassemble to discuss and debate their findings as a whole class. We usually begin by writing "Values early in the story" and "Values at or near the end" on the board or projecting them from a computer.

We then ask each group for its top three and bottom three values at the beginning and at the end. As the groups report, we list their choices. While many of the groups have similar values in the top and bottom three rankings, there is never complete agreement.

Students debate their ideas in a whole-class discussion. As the groups compare answers and discuss why they ranked Mama's values the way they did, the discussion is at a high level because of their previous work. In order to argue that one value is more important than another, students must look to the text to support their interpretations. We need to do little more to create a lively discussion than to encourage students to present their rankings, evidence, and reasoning to support their viewpoints about Mama's values and how they should be ranked. Many students are eager to participate and defend their views.

Whether students ultimately reach a consensus is not important. After all, ambiguity or complexity is what makes literature—and life—more interesting and challenging. However, it is important for students to support their ideas with textual evidence and possibly refine or change them based on others' ideas. This activity helps students draw inferences about Mama and focus upon why and how her values change. Ultimately the activity helps students understand the meaning of the story.

The many possible choices built into the design of the activity make it potentially useful for any literary work in which a major character undergoes a change, coming-of-age, or maturing process. In fact, with some modification, it also may be used in analyzing a static as well as a dynamic character. For example, Dee in "Everyday Use" does not change or only changes superficially. Having students identify the static nature of a character such as Dee and discuss whether a change is genuine or not is also important.

If the activity is being used to examine a complex character in a longer work, such as Huck Finn, then we might add one or two blanks on the "Character Analysis" sheet and ask students to rank the character's top and bottom four or five values at the beginning and end of the work, or we might also ask students to assess Huck's values at various points in the novel. For example, having students examine Huck's values after he decides not to turn Jim in to the men hunting for escaped slaves provides students with an opportunity to gain insight into how and why Huck's values change once he is forced to make an important moral choice. This process helps students better understand the profound changes in Huck's values at the end of the novel when he rejects civilization and decides to "light out for the Territory ahead of the rest."

While the "Analyzing Values" sheet contains a fairly comprehensive list of terms and definitions, teachers may need to review the choices in light of the specific text their students are reading. For example, we have added "Conformity/Order—Desiring an adherence to the status quo; resisting change to the established order" for use with *Huckleberry Finn,* because of Aunt Sally's attempts to "sivilize" Huck or get him to conform to society's values and mores. Certainly the number of choices given and the choices themselves can vary depending upon the ages and skill levels of students and the works being studied. However, it is important to make sure that there are contrasting, arguable choices of values for students to consider. A key to the success of the activity is that students argue and wrestle with different possible values.

At this point, one possible follow-up writing activity is to have students write a paragraph explaining why one value is more or less important than another value to the character of Mama, Huck Finn, or some other character. As an alternative, students might do some blogging on this topic. If there is considerable disagreement in the class discussion about the character's top and/or bottom values, then blogging offers students the opportunity to extend the classroom discussion. We prompt students to focus on the values that were controversial in class discussion and to present evidence from the text and explanations why the value they have selected is more important to the character than other possible choices. Students might also examine the values of another character from the text under consideration and discuss the top and/or bottom values of this new character and why they would rank them they way they did. Not only do these new tasks continue the discussion and debate outside the classroom, but they give students additional practice in making inferences and supporting and explaining their inferences about a literary character.

Identifying Parallels: Collecting and Analyzing Evidence

After completing the "Analyzing a Character" activity, students are ready to extend their knowledge with some additional work on finding and analyzing evidence. In this activity, we ask students to look for patterns of evidence to support a claim regarding a character's values. The first step is to assign students to look for two pieces of evidence related to the character in question. If students have just completed the character values activity with Walker's "Everyday Use" (2007), then we ask them to look for two pieces of evidence related to the character of Mama that share a common element: a repeated word or phrase, a similar action, or a similar idea (value). Students can be asked to work individually or in pairs.

For example, one of our students found two pieces of evidence in which Mama admires Dee's physical appearance. Another student selected two pieces of evidence due to their similar wording, "I didn't ask" and "I didn't want to bring up." Regarding Dee/Wangero and her male companion, Mama comments, "They didn't tell me, and I didn't ask, whether Wangero [Dee] had really gone and married him" (p. 1095); then, later, when Dee responds that Maggie can't fully appreciate the quilts that Dee now wants, Mama thinks, "I didn't want to bring up how I had offered Dee (Wangero) a quilt when she went away to college" (p. 1097).

Whether students have found evidence parallels in pairs or individually, the next step is to write some of the parallel quotes on the board or to project them. Next we lead a class discussion. In discussing, for example, what the previous evidence suggests, one student observed, "Both pieces of evidence suggest that Mama values peace. She doesn't want to bring up any comment that might cause conflict with Dee." Yet another student viewed these quotations as evidence that Mama sees but won't admit to the lack of family values in Dee's actions: Dee doesn't bother to tell her mother important details of her life, and she hasn't always treasured family heirlooms.

Certainly, two pieces of evidence may support more than one claim, depending upon the explanation or warrant the student provides. It is important to encourage students to delve more deeply into the evidence: to focus on keywords within the evidence, to identify what the author might be suggesting about the story as a whole through the evidence, and to determine how the literal evidence might work metaphorically to suggest an emotional truth or an important idea. We continue the discussion, going over student examples to ensure that they have a good sense of what constitutes strong evidence to support a claim about one of Mama's values. From this activity, our students begin to see the importance of patterns of evidence. As with the previous activity, we have done this activity in the same manner with a major character from a longer work, such as Huck in *The Adventures of Huckleberry Finn*.

One possible follow-up activity is for students to write a paragraph in which a claim regarding one of Mama's important values (or Huck's important values if students are reading *The Adventures of Huckleberry Finn*) is supported by at least two pieces of specific evidence from the text.

Explaining Evidence: The Warrant Connection

In their writing, students often omit warrants and assume that the evidence "speaks for itself." This activity provides one way to help students see that they need to explain how evidence supports a conclusion. Building on the previous activity, this activity gives students additional practice in looking closely at an author's individual word choices and putting their observations about those choices into writing. This activity utilizes the "Chalk Talk" strategy, a close reading strategy from Project CRISS (Santa, 2004) first encountered during the Teaching East Asian Literature in the High School Workshop (July 18–24, 2004, Indiana University, Bloomington, Indiana). It is a good way to look closely at an author's individual word choice and syntax and to help students turn their observations into effective warrants.

Working once again with Walker's "Everyday Use" (2007), we begin by placing a key piece of evidence on the board. Mama's comment, "I did something I never had done before: hugged Maggie to me, then dragged her on into the room, snatched the quilts out of Miss Wangero's hands and dumped them into Maggie's lap" (1098), is a good choice because it alerts the reader to a change in Mama. Thus, students are practicing close reading with a piece of evidence important in establishing the cause of Mama's change in values. Writing the evidence across two or three boards is a good idea in order to give students room to maneuver. The rules of the strategy are simple: students are not allowed to talk; no more than three students may be up at the board at one time; and using chalk (or, in the case of a white board, an appropriate marker), students may make an observation or connection, ask a question, or give a definition regarding the quote. They may also do the same for any comments. We extend the silent part of this activity as long as it seems useful. Depending on the size of the class, the teacher might require that all students participate at least once or that students limit themselves to one comment each. This is a good activity for giving even quiet students a "voice" and for tracking and building upon ideas. As one of our students observed, "It's a visual record of our ideas."

A typical blackboard will look much like a graffiti-covered wall on a city street, but the graffiti in this case consists of students' observations, connections, questions, definitions, and comments. Often students make insightful observations and connections regarding the quotations. In addition, there are sometimes trails of observations and comments that respond to the observations in a kind of dialogue about a quotation or part of a quotation. Some of the observations and comments may be contradictory, which help students see that the warrant, the explanation, is essential in order to connect the quotation to a claim about a character and that character's values.

In essence, the "Chalk Talk" sets the stage for a whole-class discussion of students' observations and that is the next step in the activity: we lead a whole-class discussion of what students have written on the board. We ask questions such as, "What idea would you like to discuss further?" "What word would you identify as most significant within the quotation/evidence and why?" "How do you explain any contradictory observations regarding the quotation/evidence?" "What is this evidence telling you about the character?"

After the chalk talk and whole-class discussion, we have students work on the "Explaining Differences within Similarities" activity sheet (see Handout 2.14, p. 63). It is worthwhile to have them work in heterogeneous pairs or small groups, with stronger students assisting those who are less confident so that both practice and modeling take place. In constructing the activity sheet, it is sometimes useful to use sets of quotations that students have found in doing the previous activity, "Identifying Parallels," or other sets of quotations that have a level of similarity and also interesting differences to explore. Often, identifying differences within a broad similarity will help students see subtle changes that are taking place within a character, an important recognition in interpreting a complex implied relationship.

After students have completed writing their statements and explanations on the activity sheet (see Handout 2.14, p. 63), the next step is to have them exchange their responses with others in the class in order to see how their classmates interpreted and explained the data (quotations). We have each pair or small group exchange its responses with another pair or group and ask everyone to give written feedback on the quality of the written claim, the interpretation of the evidence, and the warrant (explanation of how the evidence supports the claim).

As students work through each set, they make some interesting discoveries. For example, in Set A, some students focus on how Mama moves from question to statement to command in her responses to Dee. As a result, they make a claim that the differences show how Mama becomes increasingly assertive in response to Dee's possession of the quilts. In Set B, students note the changing ways Mama refers to her daughter, first as "Miss Wangero," then as "Dee," and finally as "she." These changes may suggest Mama's growing alienation from her daughter, thus helping to explain her shift in values.

As a next step, the pairs or small groups return the activity sheets to the authors with comments. We then sometimes have a brief discussion, asking some groups to read their claims and warrants aloud so that the class has an opportunity to hear some of the best claims and warrants for each set of quotations. This also gives us an opportunity to determine how well students are mastering this difficult but important skill. If students are still having some difficulty, we might give them some additional practice with other sets of quotations.

Using the "Chalk Talk" strategy and having students work through an "Explaining Differences within Similarities" activity sheet for a major character from a longer work, such as *The Adventures of Huckleberry Finn*, can be very effective as well. Doing these activities as students read the novel, examining parts they have already read, can help them better understand how a character's values change.

What If . . . ? Character Questionnaire

This activity has a number of purposes. First, it gives students some additional practice in interpreting simple and complex implied relationships. From their initial inferences, students gather and select evidence and explain how evidence supports an interpretation about a major character. Another purpose of this activity is to overcome one of the most difficult problems teachers encounter when focusing on longer works of literature. It can be very difficult to keep students interested in a longer work, and they sometimes have trouble relating to or making connections with the characters in the work.

As discussed in Chapter I, Theory and Research, and pointed out by McCann, Johannessen, Kahn, and Flanagan (2006), one reason class discussion of literary works, especially initial discussions, may fail to elicit much student response is that questions may be beyond student capabilities or skill levels. Students may feel intimidated by the questions and are afraid to respond or provide only a superficial brief answer. This activity utilizes a familiar format, that of multiple-choice questions. But do not be deceived by the format; this activity is anything but a test. One purpose of the format is to start with something that students feel comfortable with—the multiple-choice format.

The multiple-choice questionnaire contains ten to twenty questions that focus on a single major character. The questions are designed to take the character out of the context of the story and put him or her in new situations. Students are to make their choices based on evidence from the text. The questionnaire in Handout 2.15 (p. 65) is designed to be used with the character of Huck Finn (adapted from Johannessen, 1993). This activity can be easily adapted for major characters in other literary works.

It is best to do this activity once the students are half to three-fourths of the way through a major work. Attempting to do it too soon is a problem because students haven't seen the character enough to be able to have enough to work with. We pass out the questionnaire to students and have them complete it on the basis of their understanding of the character. Then we divide the class into small groups and have them try to reach a consensus on their answers. This usually will not be a simple task since the multiple-choice questions are not designed in a typical fashion. No *one* answer is *the* correct answer for a given question. For most questions, several of the possible answers might be reasonably defended. The questions are deliberately designed to create disagreement so that students must actively engage in making inferences, gathering and selecting evidence, and explaining evidence as they argue their choices.

For example, question 4 usually creates considerable debate. Some of our students argue that Huck would give the money back immediately, citing his innocent honesty about most things, including the fact that he believes he will go to hell because he lied to the men who were looking for escaped slaves and told them that Jim was not black. Others argue that he would ask one of his friends, Jim or Tom Sawyer, what to do for the same reason and because he believes that they have wisdom about such matters. Still others say that he would close the account and move away but he would use the money so that he and Jim could escape to a free state where they could live in peace and freedom. Finally, some students even argue that Huck would likely say nothing and keep the money out of fear that if his Pap found out, he would take it from Huck and do something evil with it and maybe even abuse Huck for not giving the money to him immediately.

At the conclusion of the small-group discussion, we have students reconvene as an entire class. As they discuss each question, disagreements often arise; as they debate back and forth, they draw conclusions based on evidence from the novel.

One of the strengths of this activity is how easy it is to modify for other characters in major works. Question 3, for example, is one that we have used, slightly modified, with the characters of Jim and Tom Sawyer, and we have used a similar question for the character of Brutus in William Shakespeare's *Julius Caesar*. More important, one of the strengths of the activity is that the questions take students outside the experience of the novel or play, and they are encouraged to explore, defend, and elaborate their unique ideas. For example, for many students, the characters come alive as they make connections between characters in the novel and real people and events identified in question 11 or other questions.

The questionnaire for Huck asks students to discuss the questions orally and then to write their explanation for why they selected each response. In this way, the groups come to the whole-class discussion with something written in which they have a stake. Here is a typical exchange during a whole-class discussion of question 11:

Student 1: I think he [Huck] would most admire Cindy Sheehan because she stands up for what she believes in . . .

Student 2: Yeah, like when Huck tells the men searching for runaway slaves that the man on his raft is white.

Student 1: I wrote down that he stands up for his beliefs when he lies to the men looking for runaway slaves. They tell Huck that they are going to have to see for themselves if the man on his raft is black or white, and he talks them into believing that his Dad is sick with smallpox to scare them away. So he takes action to stand up for his beliefs and protect Jim from harm. He does more than just talk.

Student 2: So, Huck and Cindy Sheehan both take action—she not only speaks out against the war in Iraq, but she also gets other people involved and then holds vigils near the Bush ranch in Texas to protest the war.

Student 3: You might be right, but I think he would most admire Oprah Winfrey and not Sheehan.

In this excerpt, students are involved in discussing why they believe Huck would admire Cindy Sheehan or Oprah Winfrey. Exchanges like this one often go on for many minutes and become quite animated as students discuss and debate their choices and present evidence and reasoning to support their views. It may well be that because students are able to go outside the experience of the novel that they feel comfortable exploring, defending, and elaborating their ideas. In addition, these students point to evidence from the text to support their views and offer explanations of how their evidence supports their interpretations. This is exactly what we want students to learn and practice in this sequence of activities.

As a follow-up writing practice, we have students select one of the questions and write a paragraph explaining which of the answers would best fit the character and why. It is important to stress the need for evidence from the text and a clear explanation of how their evidence supports their conclusion. In this way, students are making inferences about the character (simple and complex implied relationships), drawing conclusions from those inferences, and turning their conclusions into written analyses.

Once students have worked with a questionnaire, one interesting variation is to have students make up questions, or perhaps even whole questionnaires, for other characters.

Character Values Composition

At this point, most students are ready for a more independent activity in which they must use what they have learned in the previous activities. One possible culminating writing assignment is to have students compare and contrast the values of two major characters. In the case of *Huckleberry Finn*, students might compare the values of Jim and Tom to determine which would make a better friend and why. In the case of Walker's "Everyday Use," students might compare the values of the two sisters, Maggie and Dee, to determine which is the best daughter and why or which has lived her life best according to her heritage and why.

Another possible assignment is to have students write a composition focusing on the values of a single character. For example, students might determine what Huck Finn values most early in the novel and then decide what his values are at the end of the novel. If they decide that Huck's values change, the students should give reasons and evidence for the cause of the change.

Still another approach is to have students write about a short story that they have not seen before. There are a number of possibilities, including Alice Munro's "The Red Dress," John Updike's "A&P," Richard Wright's "Almos' a Man," Nicolai Chukovski's "The Bridge," and Sherwood Anderson's "I'm a Fool." Students write a composition arguing what the main character values at the beginning of the story and at the end, whether the character's values change, and what causes them to change or remain constant. The sample assignment and planning sheet (see Handout 2.16, p. 67) are based on this possible assignment.

If a particular class or perhaps students within a class are not quite ready to analyze a story completely on their own, then the teacher might ask students to write about another character that they have not analyzed in a story they have studied. For example, after having worked with the character Mama, students might write about either Dee or Maggie from Walker's "Everyday Use" and determine if her values change from the beginning to the end of the story, and if so, how and why, and if not, why not.

Students use the "Composition Planning Sheet" (see Handout 2.16, p. 67), which contains the reading assignment and additional instruction for planning and writing a composition. Once students have read the story, we usually have them do the character analysis sheet on their own.

However, if they have some trouble, we might have students meet and discuss their findings in small groups and perhaps lead a whole-class discussion of their findings, listing them on the board for students to use when they plan their compositions.

We often have students start working on their planning sheets in class, monitor them as they work, help those who need assistance, and then assign students to finish their planning sheets for the next day. When they bring in their completed planning sheets the following day, we look them over and/or lead a brief class discussion of what they have done. If students all seem to be on the right track, we answer any questions they might have and have them get started on their compositions. The planning sheet is structured to enable students to write their compositions directly from it. At the end of the class period, we tell students when their rough drafts are due and that they will need to bring their planning sheets along with their rough drafts to class.

Revising Character Values Composition

When students bring their rough drafts to class, we have them critique their compositions in small groups, pairs, or individually. One strategy is to use the "Check Sheet" (see Handout 2.17, p. 69) to help students focus on what they have learned in the sequence of activities.

It is best to do the activity in small groups. With drafts in hand, students move to their assigned small groups. We distribute enough sheets for each member of the group. The groups read each paper aloud, and the students in the group fill out one sheet for each paper they read. We encourage students to include notes and comments explaining their responses. Once a paper has been read and the group has completed a check sheet, they attach the check sheet to the paper and return it to the writer. Then they read the second paper aloud, evaluate it as a group, attach the sheet to the paper, return it to the writer, and so on until they have read and evaluated all the papers in their group.

The check sheet method offers some distinct advantages for peer evaluation. First, it guides students' attention to the key features required for a strong paper of literary analysis. Second, the writer hears and participates in the discussion of his or her writing and develops a clear understanding of its strengths and weaknesses. If students hear two, three, or four other papers, then they will be more likely to have an understanding of what needs to be done to improve their own composition based on what was encountered in the others in their small group.

Once all rough drafts have been assessed and returned, students look over their check sheets and make revisions based on the feedback they received from their peers. As a final step in the activity, students might share their revised compositions with other students. They might read them aloud in small groups or to the whole class. Having students share their compositions underscores the idea that writing is an act of communicating ideas to an audience. It also can be an opportunity for students to reexamine their conclusions about the text. After students have shared their compositions, it is interesting to lead a class discussion focusing on what new ideas and insights they learned from hearing other students' essays, and how what they learned changed or gave further support to their interpretations of the text.

A Model Character Analysis Composition

After engaging in this sequence of activities, students tend to write some fairly sophisticated compositions. In analyzing a character, many students come upon insights into the central meaning of the story, novel, or play. In short, their writing shows how using a series of activities, such as the ones we have described, enables students to dig deeply into the literature. It also shows how such a series of activities can provide students with the extended practice that Smith and Hillocks (1988) say is necessary if students are to have the "in-depth knowledge of concepts . . . and discourse conventions" that will enable them "to mature as readers" (p. 48), and, as Johannessen (1993) argues, mature as writers.

The following composition, written by one of our sophomore students who engaged in a series of activities like the ones described in this sequence, illustrates the quality of writing that can be produced.

This particular composition focuses on the character of Dee in Alice Walker's short story "Everyday Use" and works well as a model student composition that students might examine before writing a composition on their own.

From Dee to Wangero: Is She True to Her Heritage?

Heritage is something that is passed down from preceding generations. It is also an important theme in Alice Walker's short story "Everyday Use." It is the story of a successful urban daughter, Dee, and her relationship with her less successful rural mother and sister, Maggie. In her youth and teenage years, Dee is embarrassed by her heritage. Later, she superficially values her heritage but does not understand it. As a consequence, Mama and Maggie lose a great deal of respect for her.

Initially, Dee is embarrassed by her heritage. First, her mother, who serves as the narrator says, "I am the way my daughter would want me to be: a hundred pounds lighter, my skin like an uncooked barley pancake" (1). According to Mama, Dee is not happy with the way her mother actually is. She wishes her mother could be someone different. Mama also believes that Dee is ashamed of her dark skin because she wants her mother's skin to be the creamy white color of an "uncooked barley pancake." Dee's mother is the most direct link with her heritage and she is embarrassed by her. Second, Mama recalls a letter that Dee wrote from college. She remembers her writing "no matter where we 'choose' to live, she will manage to see us. But she will never bring her friends" (2). Dee does not say she will forget about her family altogether because she will "manage" to see them. She is embarrassed by where her family lives, so embarrassed that she will "never bring her friends." Her house is where she grew up, another direct link to her heritage, and again, she is embarrassed by it. Last, Mama remembers offering Dee quilts before she went to college. She says, " . . . I had offered Dee (Wangero) a quilt when she went away to college. Then she had told me they were old-fashioned, out of style" (5). Mama acts generously by offering Dee the heirloom quilts, but she refuses them. The quilts are a tool to help her remember her heritage, but Dee shrugs it off and tells her mom that the quilts are "old-fashioned, out of style" because she would be too embarrassed for people to see that she had old quilts that weren't in style. Throughout her childhood and young adulthood, Dee does not accept her heritage but when she comes back to visit Mama and Maggie, something has obviously changed.

Later, Dee superficially values her heritage but does not understand it. First, Dee decides to change her name to Wangero, an African name, and Mama asks her why. She responds, "I couldn't bear it any longer, being named after the people who oppressed me" (3). Here, Dee is thinking that she was not named after black people but after white people, the people who "oppress" her. Ironically, while she is trying to be true to her heritage, she does not have enough knowledge of her heritage to know that she was named after her aunt Dicie, not white people who "oppress" her. Second, when Dee gets out of the car, Mama recalls, she took pictures of "me sitting there in front of the house with Maggie cowering behind me. She never takes a shot without making sure the house is included . . . . Then she puts the Polaroid in the back seat of the car, and comes up and kisses me on the forehead" (3). Before, Dee was embarrassed by her house and her family. Now, she is taking pictures of them so she can show them off to her friends. She made sure Maggie, Mama, and the house were in every shot because she wanted to show off her heritage. What strikes the reader as bizarre about this passage is that Dee does not greet her mother with a kiss until after she is finished taking pictures. If she truly cared about her family and heritage, she would have been so excited to see her mom, after a long time away that she would have kissed her mother immediately after leaving the car. Last, while Dee is trying to convince Mama to give her the quilts that she refused before she left for college, she says, "These are all pieces of dresses Grandma used to wear. She did all the stitching by hand. Imagine!" (5). Dee is fascinated that these quilts were made "by hand" because this makes them more authentic and reminds her of her heritage. This is in contrast to her previous attitude about the quilts, that they were "old-fashioned" and "out of style." She admires these quilts and is intrigued by them. Her views of the quilts are also a contrast from Maggie's. Instead of superficially admiring the quilts, Maggie actually learns how to make quilts. Similarly, instead of superficially valuing her heritage, she actually understands it. During her visit with her mother and sister, Dee superficially values her heritage but has much less understanding of it than even her sister.

Consequently, Maggie and Mama lose a lot of respect for her. First, Dee desperately begs her mother to give her the quilts but Mama says, "I . . . hugged Maggie to me, then dragged her on into the room, snatched the quilt out of Miss Wangero's hands, and dumped them into Maggie's lap" (5). Mama has a choice: give the quilts to Dee or give the quilts to Maggie. Her choice to give them to Maggie instead of Dee sends a message to Dee that a great deal of respect that her mother had for her has been lost. Mama does not refer to her daughter as Dee but as "Miss Wangero," which implies unfamiliarity toward her. Second, Mama did not leave her daughter empty-handed. She said to her, "Take one or two of the others" (5). Mama seems to not care as much about Dee anymore. She does not care if she takes "one or two." She only cares that Maggie gets the handmade quilts. She lets Dee take the "others," implying that she thinks Maggie is more important and that she has lost her respect for Dee. Last, Dee storms out of the house and tells Maggie and Mama that they don't understand their heritage. Mama recalls, "Maggie smiled, maybe at the sunglasses. But a real smile, not scared" (5). Before, Maggie was almost intimidated by her sister but after realizing how fake her sister has become, she simply "smiles" at her sister's advice. She has gotten over fearing her sister and she was "not scared" when she smiled. Previously, Maggie and Mama were intimidated by Dee and felt they were inferior to her, but after her visit, they realize that they are not inferior because they understand their heritage more that she does.

Heritage played a large role in the way that Dee was trying to live her life. She starts out embarrassed by her heritage. Eventually, she begins to value her heritage but only superficially which makes Mama and Maggie view her negatively. Heritage plays a key role in many people's lives but when one wears it on his or her shoulder and does not truly understand it, others see right through their transparent costume and that person's integrity is often questioned.

—Daniel Hornung

Handout 2.11. Analyzing Values

What do you value most? What do you value least? What do the characters in the text value? Here are some possibilities:

Friendship	Spending time with friends; having close friends; being a good friend; helping and supporting your friends; maintaining friendships over time.
Financial Security	Having enough money; doing well financially; being financially secure.
Career/Work	Having a career you enjoy; advancing in your career; being successful in your work.
Family	Spending time with family; being close to your family; marriage; raising children.
Appearance	Looking your best; being attractive to others.
Achievement	Being successful; accomplishing one's goals; being highly skilled.
Health	Having good health; keeping in good shape; being physically fit.
Social Acceptance	Being well-liked by others; having many friends; being popular.
Education	Having or getting a good education; doing well in school; being intelligent.
Having Fun	Being able to do things that are enjoyable to you; participating in recreational activities; having a good time.
Respect	Being respected by others; being treated with respect.
Adventure/ Excitement	Doing things that involve excitement or daring; doing things that are different and/or unusual.
Religion	Serving God or a Supreme Being; living according to your religious beliefs.
Peace	Feeling safe and secure; being able to live without fear; not having to deal with a lot of pain, conflict, and/or fighting.
Power	Having influence over others; being looked up to by others; being in charge; being in control; being seen as strong and influential.
Independence	Having freedom to make your own decisions; being able to do things the way you want to; being able to do things for yourself without having to depend on others.
Service to Others	Helping others; making the world a better place; using your abilities to help other people.
Integrity	Doing the right thing because it is right; standing up for what is right.
Honesty	Telling the truth; being open with others; being yourself; not hiding the truth or hiding from the truth; not putting on an act.
Creativity	Being creative and/or artistic; using your imagination; being able to express your uniqueness.
Fairness/Equality	Treating all people fairly and equally; accepting differences; working to see that others' rights are not violated.
Wisdom	Having knowledge and good judgment; making good decisions.
Others?	loyalty _____ _____ _____

Writing about Literature, 2nd ed., Revised and Updated by Larry Johannessen, Elizabeth A. Kahn, and Carolyn Calhoun Walter © 2009 NCTE.

Handout 2.12. What Are Your Values?

Directions: Using the list of values, rank your top four and bottom four values in order and predict what you think the top four and bottom four values will be for the class as a whole.

Your Values (Top four in rank order)	Your Class' Values (Predicted top four in order)	Your Class' Values (Actual top four in order)
1. Family	1. respect	1.
2. friendship	2. friendship	2.
3. Integrity	3. honesty	3.
4. Honesty	4. ~~education~~ integrity	4.

Your Values (Bottom four in rank order)	Your Class' Values (Predicted bottom four in order)	Your Class' Values (Actual bottom four in order)
19. career	19. career	19.
20. power	20. appearance	20.
21. religion	21. power	21.
22. Appearance	22. religion	22.

Be prepared to explain why you ranked your values as you did and why you ranked the class' values as you did.

Writing about Literature, 2nd ed., Revised and Updated by Larry Johannessen, Elizabeth A. Kahn, and Carolyn Calhoun Walter © 2009 NCTE.

Handout 2.13. Character Analysis

Character Analyzed: __Momma__

	Character's values early in the work	*If the character's values change, what are they at or near the end*
What does the character value *most*? List his or her top three values *in order*.	1. family 2. respect 3. ~~peace~~ career/work	1. respect 2. family 3. peace
What does the character value *least*? List his or her bottom three values in order.	20. appearance 21. having fun 22. education	20. appearance 21. having fun 22. education

Be prepared to present **reasons** and **evidence** from the literary work to support your choices.

Handout 2.14. Explaining Differences within Similarities

Directions: For each quotation below, circle one or two keywords or phrases. In addition, consider not only what is said but how it is said. Mark up the quotations as much as you can by following the chalk-talk model. For both sets of evidence (A and B), a similarity is stated. Looking for differences within a similarity often yields interesting results. What differences do you see among the quotes within each set? After you have marked up each set of quotations, write a statement about Mama's values that is suggested by a significant difference you've identified in the space provided. You may want to refer to the "Analyzing Values" sheet you used earlier. Then, in one or more sentences below each quotation, explain *how* the evidence supports your stated claim regarding the differences you've identified.

A. Statement regarding similarity: Mama responds to Dee's repeated requests regarding the quilts.

Claim regarding difference (change in Mama):

_____

_____

1. When Dee/Wangero first asks Mama for "these old quilts," Mama responds, "Why don't you take one or two of the others?" (p. 1096).

_____

_____

_____

2. When Dee still wants the quilts, Mama responds, "The truth is . . . I promised to give them quilts to Maggie, for when she marries John Thomas" (p. 1097).

_____

_____

_____

3. After Dee still insists on keeping the quilts and Mama forcibly takes them from her, Mama remarks to Dee, "Take one or two of the others" (p. 1098).

_____

_____

_____

continued on next page

B. Statement regarding similarity: Mama takes a stand against her older daughter and recalls her reactions.

Claim regarding difference (change in Mama):

_____

_____

1. Mama recounts that she "snatched the quilts from out of Miss Wangero's hands and dumped them in Maggie's lap" (p. 1098).

_____

_____

_____

2. When Mama tells Dee to take the other quilts, Mama recalls that she "said [this statement] to Dee" (p. 1098).

_____

_____

_____

3. As Dee leaves their confrontation, Mama recounts that "she turned without a word" (p. 1098). After this, until the end of the story, Mama never refers to Dee by name; Mama only refers to "she" (p. 1098).

_____

_____

_____

Handout 2.15. What if Huck Finn . . . ? Character Questionnaire

Directions: Read each of the following statements and circle the letter that best completes the statement in terms of what you think would fit the character of Huck Finn. Be prepared to defend your answers with reasoning based on evidence from the novel. Below each statement, write a brief explanation of your reasoning. Use evidence from the text to support your answers.

1. If Huck were at a music concert, he would
   A. stand in the back by himself   C. stand right next to the speakers
   B. be the drummer in the band   D. harass the band to get backstage passes
Explanation:

2. If Huck were at a baseball game, he would
   A. be a player   C. be an umpire
   B. be a manager   D. be a fan who harasses players, coaches, and umpires
Explanation:

3. If Huck were alive today, his job or profession would most likely be a/an
   A. anchorperson on the local evening news   C. independent repair man/carpenter
   B. farmer/rancher   D. detective
Explanation:

4. If Huck's bank made an error and gave him an extra three thousand dollars, he probably would
   A. say nothing and keep the money   C. give the money back immediately
   B. ask his best friend if he should keep D. close out his account and move
      the money   away
Explanation:

5. On a typical date Huck would take his date to
   A. a NASCAR race   C. a dance
   B. an amusement park   D. the zoo
Explanation:

6. If Huck were involved in a minor car accident, he would probably get out of his car and say,
   A. "This was your fault."   C. "This was no one's fault."
   B. "This was my fault."   D. "Let's forget about this."
Explanation:

continued on next page

7. If Huck were at a party, he would probably
    A. drink too much and make a fool of himself
    B. stand quietly in the corner and people-watch
    C. flirt with all of the girls
    D. tell everyone that he will host the next party tomorrow night
Explanation:

8. Huck's favorite hobby would most likely be
    A. playing cards   C. reading
    B. hiking alone   D. listening to music
Explanation:

9. Huck's favorite type of movie would be
    A. a horror film   C. a comedy
    B. a science-fiction movie   D. a dramatic film
Explanation:

10. If Huck were alive today, he would most likely live
    A. in a house in the suburbs   C. in an apartment in the city
    B. on a farm in the country   D. with no permanent address
Explanation:

11. Huck would most admire
    A. Michael Moore   C. Oprah Winfrey
    B. Lance Armstrong   D. Cindy Sheehan
Explanation:

12. In school Huck's favorite "subject" would be
    A. applied technology   C. biology
    B. history   D. lunch/passing periods
Explanation:

Writing about Literature, 2nd ed., Revised and Updated by Larry Johannessen, Elizabeth A. Kahn, and Carolyn Calhoun Walter © 2009 NCTE.

Handout 2.16. Composition Planning Sheet

Assignment: Read the short story you have been assigned and write a composition in which you explain how the main character's values change and why. First fill out the "Character Analysis" for the character's values.

Character's top value at the beginning of the story:_____

List **specific** evidence for the character's top value at the beginning of the story.

EVIDENCE	EXPLANATION of how the evidence supports the claim

Character's top value at or near the end of the story:_____

List **specific** evidence for the character's top value at or near the end of the story.

EVIDENCE	EXPLANATION of how the evidence supports the claim

continued on next page

Explain what **causes** this change in values. List supporting evidence for this change.

EVIDENCE	EXPLANATION of how the evidence supports the claim

Your thesis statement might explain what he or she values most at the beginning, what he or she values most at the end, and the reason(s) for the change in values.

Sample Thesis
At the beginning of "Everyday Use," Mama values peace with Dee, but as Mama sees the cost of this peace for Maggie, Mama begins to value integrity.

YOUR THESIS:

_____

_____

_____

Writing about Literature, 2nd ed., Revised and Updated by Larry Johannessen, Elizabeth A. Kahn, and Carolyn Calhoun Walter © 2009 NCTE.

Handout 2.17. Check Sheet

s: Write the name of the author of the composition in the appropriate space
the names of the evaluators in the appropriate spaces. As you read the
tion, discuss it with your partner(s) and circle the appropriate response to
uestion, 1–7. Include comments to explain your responses.

he of Writer _____

me of Evaluator(s) _____

_____

_____

1. Does the writer have a clearly stated thesis that follows the directions of the assignment?	YES	NO
2. Does the writer provide at least two pieces of specific, convincing evidence for the character's top values at the beginning?	YES	NO
3. Does the writer clearly explain *how* each piece of evidence supports her/his thesis?	YES	NO
4. Does the writer explain the reason(s) for the character's change in values?	YES	NO
5. Does the writer provide specific evidence to support what she/he gives as reasons for the change?	YES	NO
6. Does the writer provide at least two pieces of specific, convincing evidence for the character's top value at the end?	YES	NO
7. Does the writer clearly explain *how* each piece of evidence supports her/his thesis?	YES	NO

8. Reread the paper and mark any places where you think the writer needs to correct spelling, punctuation, capitalization, usage, etc.

9. What arguments can you think of that might be used *against* this writer's thesis?

Writing about Literature, 2nd ed., Revised and Updated by Larry Johannessen, Elizabeth A. Kahn, and Carolyn Calhoun Walter © 2009 NCTE.

Interpreting an Author's Generalization Sequence: Romantic Love

In this sequence students practice the skills necessary for interpreting and writing compositions concerning an author's generalization. Since dealing with an author's generalizations requires students to interpret simple and complex implied relationships, teachers need to determine—perhaps through inventories, or previous instruction—whether students are ready for instruction at this level. Even if they are, it is likely that work at this level, especially with more complex novels and plays, would be preceded by discussion and activities at less complex levels of the reading hierarchy.

Although this sequence focuses on the theme of romantic love and marriage, any focus—courage, fear, memory, friendship, coming-of-age, war and peace, etc.—might be chosen for a group of literary works. Through in-depth focus on a single concept in several works, students develop greater precision and perception in interpreting authors' generalizations. The activities lead students through increasingly sophisticated texts as they progress from interpreting cartoons and love-related myths and fables to interpreting poems and plays. The final activities focus on William Shakespeare's *The Tragedy of Romeo and Juliet*, but they may be easily adapted for other works regarding love and marriage, such as *The Taming of the Shrew* or *A Midsummer Night's Dream*.

True Love Opinionnaire

In this introductory activity, students consider their own and their classmates' differing ideas of love, a major thematic concept they will encounter in the selected poems and *Romeo and Juliet*. We begin by passing out the "True Love Opinionnaire" (see Handout 2.18, p. 90) to students and asking them to complete the "You" column by agreeing or disagreeing with each statement. As with all opinionnaires, we remind students that there are no right or wrong answers, only opinions! However, opinions come from somewhere, so students should have examples, anecdotes, and reasons ready for later discussion.

Upon students' completion of the opinionnaires, an effective way to begin whole-class discussion is to compile the results on the board—how many agree and disagree with each statement—and to focus discussion on the statements for which there was the most disagreement. The resulting discussion is lively and generates considerable debate among students. Because the statements require students to take a stand and because there are no right or wrong answers, this activity ensures a lively discussion, encouraging students to express their opinions with supporting details and to challenge the opinions of others. Even normally quiet students actively participate. Furthermore, the activity provides scaffolding for students to find meaning in the literature they will be reading later.

Many of the opinionnaire statements are designed to apply to specific works in the sequence. For example, the statement "Love at first sight is possible" directly relates to *Romeo and Juliet*. In one class of ninth-grade students, a girl raised her hand and said with great conviction, "I believe in love at first sight because that's how I fell in love!" Another student added, "My mom and dad fell in love at first sight at a dance." A skeptical listener replied, "How can you fall in love at first sight? You don't even know the person." Another student agreed by saying, "You just fall in love with the person's looks if you fall in love at first sight. You don't even know the real person." In discussing the idea of love at first sight prior to reading how Shakespeare handles this idea in the play, students are thinking through how they feel about this issue and closing the gap between their experiences and the experience of the play.

The teacher's role in this kind of prereading/writing activity is not to tell students how to think about these issues, but rather to encourage them to explain and defend their viewpoints, to ensure that a variety of viewpoints is expressed and discussed, and, of course, to prompt clarification and provide synthesis when necessary and appropriate. For example, some of our students ask about the meaning of "Love is blind." When we ask other students for their ideas, they offer explanations such as "This means that love causes you not to see another's faults or potential relationship problems" and "This means that you only see the good stuff," which engenders yet further discussion.

This activity introduces students to the concepts and strategies they will be learning and practicing in the sequence. They are analyzing generalizations about love that they may encounter in their reading, and as they discuss these generalizations, they are providing supporting evidence, explaining how the evidence supports a generalization (providing warrants), and anticipating and refuting opposing viewpoints. In addition to providing scaffolding for unit ideas and skills, the format for the opinionnaire directs students to return to these statements later in their study to see how their views compare to a number of characters in *Romeo and Juliet*.

One possible follow-up writing assignment is to have students select one or more of the generalizations from the opinionnaire, perhaps one that the class could not agree upon, and write a paragraph expressing their opinion of the statement and why they think their view is more viable than the opposing viewpoint. In this way students get written practice supporting a generalization and refuting an opposing position.

The format for this opinionnaire activity may be easily adapted for any thematic concept. For example, an opinionnaire we created for *Macbeth* on the concept of manhood included statements such as "You are a man when you have power over others" and "You are a man when you have control over yourself and your actions." A successful opinionnaire typically contains ten to twenty statements, depending upon the length and difficulty of the work or works students will study, the focus of instruction, and the age and ability level of students. Opinionnaire statements are keyed to specific interpretive problems and ask students to respond "agree" or "disagree," "true" or "false," or "yes" or "no" to each statement. An effective opinionnaire will include controversial statements, encourage disagreement among students, and prompt discussion of issues central to those arising in the literature. Sometimes it is useful to include two similar statements such as 5 and 18 in the "True Love Opinionnaire": "True love is unconditional" and "Love never changes." If students did not respond similarly to both, we can then ask follow-up questions in discussion. If they responded differently to these to statements, we ask why: What differences do they see in these two statements? The goals of opinionnaire design and implementation are always to help students clarify and articulate their thinking regarding key concepts.

What's Love Got to Do with It?

As the results of NAEP (NCES 2005) indicate, interpreting authors' generalizations is difficult for secondary students. Hillocks's taxonomy (Hillocks, 1980; Hillocks & Ludlow, 1984) suggests that it is difficult because readers can only make interpretations at this level if they are able to attend to significant details and understand many stated and implied relationships within their reading. The longer and more sophisticated the literature, the more difficult this task becomes. Students often have trouble just understanding what is meant by the term "author's generalization" or even a definition such as *what the author is showing about human nature or the human condition*. Giving students the definition and examples does not ensure that they will be able to perform this skill when they read a literary work.

Beginning instruction with cartoons and other simpler literary forms, such as fables or myths, before approaching more complex works of literature helps students understand what an author's generalization is. In cartoons, even though the author's generalization is not explicitly stated, all the data are present within one picture and caption. In addition, for students who are visually oriented, cartoons provide a good starting point for working with authors' generalizations. Cartoons on the subject of love may be found on the Internet, in magazines, in newspapers, or in book collections. And, of course, cartoons on other thematic concepts from power to peace can be culled from these sources as well in order to adapt this activity to other units of instruction.

We begin the activity by passing out the "What's Love Got to Do with It" activity sheet (see Handout 2.19, p. 91), going over the directions with students and having them answer the questions individually or in pairs.

Once students are finished, we lead a class discussion focusing on their responses to the questions. As students debate their choice of statements from the opinionnaire with which the cartoonist would most agree and disagree, we encourage them to provide details from the cartoon for support. For example, some students might offer the opinion that the cartoonist is disagreeing with "Love is blind" and mention that the lady in the cartoon is looking for information rather than trying to avoid it. Other students might argue that the cartoonist would disagree with "The spiritual aspects of love are more important than the physical ones" and mention that the information one might discover about another via the Internet would most likely be superficial. After students have discussed various possibilities and details that led them to their conclusions, it usually becomes clear that there are many more choices with which the cartoonist might disagree than agree. We then ask students to work in pairs to create a one-sentence statement similar to those of the opinionnaire that summarizes what the cartoonist is showing about love or love relationships. As the pairs work, we encourage them to consider different possibilities and to go back to the drawing to evaluate each possibility, weighing choices of wording as they attempt to state clearly what the cartoonist is conveying.

Once the pairs have finished working on their generalizations, we record the responses on the board, on an overhead, or via computer projection. As a whole class, students compare the various possibilities and select what they consider to be the best option. Although there is usually some variety within the options produced, students have been known to defend vigorously the choice of a single word over another. We have had students offer possibilities such as "You can't be too careful about love," "You should enter into a relationship with your eyes wide open,"

"Knowledge is power," and "A modern relationship is based on practical considerations rather than physical or personal attraction." In evaluating the merits of each, students argue that some statements are too general or too literal while others need a little refinement. For example, some students like "A modern relationship is founded on practical considerations rather than personal attraction," because "modern" takes the computer into account and "practical considerations" takes the keyword "vet" into account. However, others argue that the woman in the picture may still disqualify her date on other grounds. Thus, they might suggest substituting "as well as" for "rather than." In doing so, students experience verbally a process that by the end of the instruction they should be doing mentally on their own—generating possible generalizations, evaluating each based on the details (evidence), and refining their ideas to achieve a clearly stated generalization of what the cartoonist (author) is suggesting about love or love relationships.

As a possible follow-up writing activity, we sometimes ask students to find a cartoon dealing with love or love relationships on their own in a newspaper, magazine, book, or from the Internet and to write a generalization that they believe expresses what the cartoonist is saying about love or love relationships. At the next class period, each student then turns in a generalization along with a copy of the cartoon. At this point, it might be worthwhile to have students exchange their cartoons and generalizations with one another for comment. Students can use the following questions to evaluate one another's generalizations: Is the generalization accurate? Is it clearly stated so that it accounts for the details in the cartoon? After receiving feedback, students have an opportunity to revise their generalizations if they wish before turning them in.

Romantic Love Myths and Fables

While the cartoon activity introduces students to what an author's generalization is and how to write one, students may need additional support and practice before they tackle more complex works of literature. Working with fables or myths in an instructional sequence before dealing with poetry, short stories, and longer works provides additional early practice for students. In fables and myths, the author's generalization— or moral or explanation of a cultural belief or practice—is often explicitly stated. Or, if it is not, the author's generalization is less subtle than in other forms of literature. [If a fable contains an explicitly stated moral or lesson, or a myth contains the explicitly stated explanation of the cultural belief, ritual, or natural phenomena that appears on the copy students are given, then a question about what the moral or lesson is would not be classified as author's generalization because it is at the literal level.]

In this activity, through developing morals for fables or the explanation of the belief or ritual that a myth illustrates, students practice stating authors' generalizations and supporting their conclusions. To prepare for this activity, we gather together a group of four or five fables or myths. Alexander Eliot's *The Universal Myths: Heroes, Gods, Tricksters, and Others* contains several multicultural myths related to love, and, of course, Edith Hamilton's *Mythology* contains a cluster of love-related myths, including "Cyx and Alcyone" and "Endymion." Another good source for myths is Bernard Evslin's *Heroes, Gods, and Monsters of the Greek Myths*. Robert Temple and Olivia Temple's *The Complete Fables (Penguin Classics)* and Aesop and Laura Gibbs's edition of *Aesop's Fables (Oxford's World Classics)* are two good collections of Aesop's fables that contain a number of fables related to love. Aesop's fables also are available on the Internet. Once we have found the fables or myths, the next step is to copy them so that the morals or lessons, if they are explicitly stated, are removed.

We begin the activity by asking students what they know about fables (or myths). For fables, students generally will mention characteristics such as the main characters usually are animals that have human characteristics and the story usually states a moral. After a brief discussion, we distribute the fable and questions that we are using. One we have often used successfully is Aesop's fable, "Venus and Cat." Because this is a fable that is not widely known, most students will not have seen it previously. The fable concerns a cat that is in love with a young man and prays to Venus for her help. In response to the cat's petition, Venus changes the cat into a young woman whom the young man immediately loves and marries. As a test of the young woman's true nature, Venus sends a mouse to the newlyweds' home. The young woman immediately pounces upon the mouse and kills it. Venus immediately changes the woman back to her original cat form. Along with the fable, we pass out the following questions:

1. What things about the cat could Venus change and what things couldn't she change? Why couldn't she change some things? [Complex implied relationship]

2. Look at the "True Love Opinionnaire." Find any statements with which you think the author of this fable would strongly agree or disagree. What in the fable leads you to your conclusions?

3. Make up a good moral for this fable. (In creating a moral, think about what the author is showing about love or love relationships or human nature.) What evidence in the fable leads you to this conclusion? [Author's generalization]

After students answer the questions on their own, we lead a class discussion focusing on their answers. As students present various possible morals, a volunteer lists these on the blackboard, whiteboard, or projection device. As students debate which statement of the moral is best, we encourage them to provide evidence from the text for support.

After this practice, students are now ready to work more independently in generating morals for other love fables. We hand out copies of two additional fables, such as Aesop's "The Lion in Love" and "The Man and His Two Wives," again with the morals omitted, and give students the following assignment:

> Read each of the following fables and think about what each author seems to be showing about love, love relationships, or human nature. Write the best moral you can for each fable and explain what evidence from the fable led you to write the moral you did.

In pairs or in small, heterogeneous groups of three to five, students work together to write a moral for each fable. As group members propose different morals, they consider various possibilities and go back to the text to evaluate each. Students weigh choices for wording, attempting to clearly state what they mean.

After all the pairs or groups have completed this step, a student from each pair or group puts on the blackboard, whiteboard, or overhead the moral his or her pair or group wrote for each fable. We then lead a class discussion of each fable by having students identify the best moral and defend their choices. Most often each pair or group will have proposed somewhat different morals. Whether the differences are slight or extreme, lively discussion ensues as students defend their choices and challenge others. They experience verbally a process that we want them to do mentally on their own—generate possible answers, evaluate them, and refine their ideas. In one class discussion, a group argued that the best moral for "The Man and His Two Wives" is "A person can never be happy with two wives." Another group disagreed and pointed out that in the story the most important thing was that both wives were ashamed of their husband. They concluded that the moral is "You should be happy with what you have instead of trying to change it." The debate continued as another group argued for another possible moral: "If you try to change something, you sometimes ruin it."

At this point, the value of designing this activity with fables that deal with a similar concept becomes clear. We can help students refine their moral for this fable by asking a question such as, "The other two fables, 'Venus and the Cat' and 'The Lion in Love,' also involve someone trying to change another; how are these fables different? In what ways would their morals be different? How could the morals be stated to emphasize these differences?" As students respond to questions like these, they refine their morals and reach a better understanding of the subtle differences in the authors' generalizations.

A possible follow-up writing assignment asks students to write a short composition stating the moral of another love fable, such as Aesop's "The Fatal Marriage," and defending their moral using evidence from the text.

By using fables in this activity, we are not trying to suggest that an author's generalization is always moralistic. To bring out this idea in later discussions of authors' generalizations in poetry or short stories, we will ask students a question such as, "How is the author's generalization in a poem (or short story) different from a moral?" In this way, students themselves discover differences in various literary forms.

Puzzling over True Love Sonnets

The idea of the "puzzle poem" originated with an activity encountered during a 1999 National Endowment for the Humanities summer workshop on "Teaching Shakespeare through Performance" in Ashland, Oregon. At the workshop, leaders gave each participant a different line from a poem by Lawrence Ferlinghetti. Through comparison and discussion, participants assembled themselves by poetry line into an order that made sense to them. The activity is modified here in order to help students inductively identify the characteristics of a sonnet.

Before starting this activity, we gather together four or five of Shakespeare's sonnets. We have often used Sonnets 18, 23, 61, 91, and 116 successfully, although others can certainly be used. Shakespeare's sonnets are available from a number of different sources, including *The Complete Signet Classic Shakespeare,* various collections of Shakespeare's poetry, general poetry collections, anthologies of literature, and the Internet.

Students work in pairs for this activity. To prepare, we cut a copy of William Shakespeare's "Sonnet 18" into fifteen individual strips (the title and each of the fourteen lines) that are then mixed randomly and placed within a large envelope. Teachers will need to make an appropriate number of envelopes ahead of time. For example, if the class has thirty students, then the teacher will need fifteen envelopes, each with fifteen strips representing the title and fourteen lines of the poem.

After dividing the class into pairs, we give each pair of students an envelope and ask them to construct a poem from the fourteen lines by using any strategies that make sense to them. As the pairs work, we circulate around the room to monitor students' progress and the methods they are using to "solve" the puzzle. Some pairs focus on sense; some use end rhyme; some use punctuation cues; some use common rhetorical patterns such as question/answer format. After ten or fifteen minutes or when some pairs have "solved" the puzzle or gotten close, we read the sonnet aloud and have students compare their work to Shakespeare's. Or, we may have pairs volunteer to read their constructed poems before reading and comparing their work to Shakespeare's. Our students have been known to prefer their poetic arrangement to the Bard's! Finally, we ask students to share the strategies they used that were helpful to them in solving the puzzle. Observations regarding rhyme scheme and content will set the stage for the next part of the lesson.

Upon completion of the class discussion, we give students copies of Sonnets 18, 29, 61, 91, and 116. Students meet in small groups to compare the five sonnets for common features and to list as many common features as they can. We ask them to look for features that apply to most or all of the sonnets, thus creating valid generalizations for their sonnet set. For example, a strong common feature statement might be "All sonnets contain fourteen lines" or "Most of the sonnets (4 of 5) specifically address a particular loved one." However, "Sonnets begin with a question" is true for only two examples and would not qualify as a valid generalization.

After groups have composed their lists of common sonnet features, we lead a class discussion of what the groups learned and compile a class list, asking for appropriate illustrations. An overhead transparency or computer projection of one sonnet can be marked to illustrate each of the features that the class lists. Together in discussion, students should inductively arrive at a fairly complete list of sonnet characteristics, including commonalities of content and form. Typical responses might include comments like those made earlier and others such as "The lines alternate end rhymes except the last two lines" or "All the poems are about love." Usually, a few students will notice the shifts within the sonnets and the "change" words that signal them: "In all the sonnets at least one line begins with *but*, *yet*, or *O, no*." Again, inductively, they are discovering the concept of "the turn" [a shift in the meaning, tone, or focus of the poem that is signaled by words such as *but*, *yet*, or *O, no*.] in a sonnet. If students do not identify important characteristics during the discovery process of class discussion, we add to the class list at the end of discussion. Usually, however, we only need to supply conventional terminology such as *couplet* or *turn* to the discussion.

Of course, we might have used less class time by just supplying the list of sonnet characteristics to students, but we have found that these concepts stay with students more readily when they have actually manipulated, constructed, and observed the data—in this case the lines and sonnets—to reach their own conclusions.

In course evaluations, students have often commented that their earlier work with Shakespearean sonnets, including activities such as this one and those that follow, aided their reading *Romeo and Juliet* by giving them practice with the play's language and concepts in a shorter format.

Analyzing an Author's (or Poet's) Generalization

Most students will need additional work with Shakespeare's sonnets before they can recognize and create valid authors' generalization statements about them. One way to assess students' reading levels with respect to the sonnets and to give students a closer look at one poem is to spend more time with Sonnet 18, especially if it was used as the "puzzle poem."

We begin with a round-robin reading of the sonnet. This works best if students are seated in a circle. Once students are in place with copies of the poem, we give the direction that the class will be reading the sonnet aloud by turns. One student will read to a hard stop [a period, colon, question mark, or semicolon] before passing to an adjacent classmate who also reads to a hard stop. Then we begin, modeling the method before passing the reading on to the student on our immediate left who will do the same and so on until the entire sonnet has been read aloud. Directing students to read in this manner models reading poetry for understanding since many students stop at the end of a poetic line rather than at the end of a thought. An oral reading also gets the sound of the language into students' ears, which further enhances their understanding. After the round-robin reading, we call on a volunteer student to read the complete sonnet aloud. After the second reading, students work individually on the questions for Sonnet 18 (see Handout 2.20, p. 92).

As students work on the questions, we circulate around the room to monitor progress and provide help when needed. Once students finish working on the questions, we lead a whole-class discussion of their responses. This gives further insight into students' level of understanding. At this point, one strategy to use is to have students add to their answers during class discussion in a different color of ink or in pen if pencil was originally used. Then we collect students' answers at the end of the discussion and look them over later to further assess students' understanding of the material and to give them credit for "listening smart" (writing things down during the discussion) as well as knowing the "right" answers. Of course, the final discussion goal is to help students interpret the poet's generalization and generate a good, clear statement of the poet's generalization about love and possibly additionally about art.

Based upon our assessments of students' comprehension levels, we use a variety of activities with Shakespeare's sonnets to help students work within their zone of proximal development—whether it is at the simple or complex inference levels—to help them move beyond these to successful author's generalization statements.

Assessing Generalizations

After students have worked collectively and individually with Sonnets 18, 29, 61, and 91 at the earlier levels of the reading hierarchy as necessary, they are prepared for more independent practice at the author's generalization level with these same sonnets. This activity presents choices to students, giving them data to examine and assess. As students discuss and debate the merits of possible poet's generalization statements, they arrive at a more sophisticated understanding of each sonnet.

Students will need their copies of the four sonnets (18, 29, 61, and 91) as well as the "Assessing Shakespeare's Generalizations" (see Handout 2.21, p. 93) activity sheet, which contains a set of four possible generalizations for each of these four sonnets. Students work in small heterogeneous groups of three to five. It is important to have a range of abilities within each group so that students who may be struggling will be able to learn from stronger students. As students work through the possible generalizations, they present arguments and evidence to explain why their choice is the better one, giving them oral practice in what they will later be asked to do in writing.

Giving students several choices forces them to assess the merits of each statement in terms of their reading of the poem rather than just to agree with the first idea someone suggests. For example, while one student may argue that "Being in love makes one feel like royalty" is a good choice for Sonnet 29 and cite the last two lines as evidence, another student will counter that the word "scorn" in the sonnet's last line actually suggests that the speaker feels superior to royalty due to his love.

After the small groups have completed their task, we bring students back together for whole-class discussion, giving them the opportunity to hear an even broader range of ideas and allowing them to further discuss, debate, and refine their own ideas as necessary. We have each group present their choice or "better option" and evidence and reasoning to support their choice. Students should be encouraged to explain and defend their differing choices and options and to offer counterarguments regarding others' choices.

Although at least one author's generalization option within each set is a viable choice, giving students the opportunity to create their own "better option" also signals to them that ideas are always open to refinement and discussion. And, in fact, students often come up with better options. For example, in assessing the generalization statement for Sonnet 61, one of our students selected "Unreturned love is a torment," citing line 10 as evidence of the speaker's torment. However, another student in her small group countered with "Thy love, though much, is not so great," saying that this line suggests an unequal love relationship and therefore "An unequal love can be disturbing" would be a better choice. Finally, the group combined the best of both students' ideas to create what they considered a "better option": "An unequal love is a torment."

One possible follow-up writing assignment is to have students write a paragraph in which they use the author's (poet's) generalization claim that they have chosen or created for one of the sonnets and support it with specific evidence from the text and explanations of how the evidence supports the claim (warrants).

For other sonnets or poems, a similar activity may be created by following the same steps we followed in originally generating the information needed to create this activity:

- Give small groups of students copies of one or more poems. Ask them to discuss what the speaker is suggesting about love (or another topic) in each poem and to write a statement that best captures their thinking.

- Collect the students' statements and assess them. Identify strong statements as well as the general types of errors being made in the weaker statements [e.g., statements that cover only part of the poem; statements that are too broad; statements that are too literal; statements that inaccurately interpret part of the poem]. We use these statements to generate choices for a handout or to provide ideas for generating similar statements of our own.

- When we have more than one class working with the same curriculum, we use statements from one class for another and vice versa. Or, we may modify the statements so that students will not recognize their own. The idea is to give students an objective set of statements from which to work. Of course, after the initial creation, the same sets may be used or modified as necessary in subsequent years without the initial steps.

Creating an activity using these steps has the benefit of identifying the particular problems that our students are having in creating good authors' generalizations and giving them practice in assessing what may be a better choice.

What Is the Best Way to Say That?

We often use students' follow-up writing assignments, such as the paragraphs generated from their writing on one of the Shakespearean sonnets in the preceding activity, not only to assess how well students are mastering the new target skills, but also to determine the rhetorical areas on which students may need to work in order to write stronger papers. Thus, we are asking students to work on form only after they have a good grasp of procedural knowledge. We might quickly read through a set of student paragraphs, giving them check, check minus, or check plus assessments related to the quality of their generalizations and use of supporting evidence. But we might also note students' common rhetorical problems and use them as the basis for an activity using "Explaining a Poet's Generalization" (see Handout 2.22, p. 94). Such quick, informative assessments ensure that students are working within their zone of proximal development.

We created the "Explaining a Poet's Generalization" activity sheet for students who understand the basic format of context, evidence, and explanation (warrant) for supporting an argument but who need further practice in integrating evidence, in quoting only what was analyzed, and in presenting analysis and explanation rather than paraphrasing. Using Graff's terminology, students ready for this activity have a working knowledge of the elaborated code of argument but would benefit from guided practice in refining their elaboration. The activity is designed so that students encounter various presentations of the same material. They decide for themselves the best choice from among those given and why that choice is best. In research cited by Hillocks (1986) on the most effective strategies for improving student writing, Troyka (1973) made use of similar criteria-guided revision and assessment activities in studies that showed the greatest gains in student writing.

To begin, we give students copies of Sonnet 116. If students have not worked with the sonnet before, we may ask them to read through the sonnet on their own several times and to look up words they do not understand. Then we have students complete the "Explaining a Poet's Generalization" activity sheet on their own for homework or in pairs or small groups in class. Either way, it is important that students individually have a stake in deciding and articulating which choices are strongest and why.

Once students have worked with the material, we lead a class discussion of their responses. As they compare and debate selections and reasons in whole-class discussion, students inductively create the criteria for more sophisticated and effective presentation as they discuss their answers and hear the opinions of others. For example, while discussing the merits of the choices for lines 5 and 6, one student may prefer response "b" for its explanation which moves beyond response "d's" paraphrase explanation or response "a's" accurate observation that lacks the explanatory link to the writer's claim stating the poet's generalization. However, another student will counter that response "c" contains response "b's" ideas expressed in a smoother manner and without the switch in pronoun to "you." At the conclusion of the discussion, we show students a copy of a model paragraph as it would look with a well-written claim (statement of an author's or poet's generalization), effective transitions, effective supporting evidence, and well-written explanations of how the evidence supports the claim. The following paragraph combines the best choices of the Sonnet 116 activity:

> The speaker of Sonnet 116 claims that true love is constant in the face of another's changes, problems, or time. In lines 2–4, the speaker claims, "Love is not love / Which alters when it alteration finds, / Or bends with the remover to remove," implying that true love will remain unchanged even if it discovers its recipient's love alters or changes. The speaker also suggests that true love is unshakable, like a lighthouse, "an ever-fixed mark," in the face of problems that arise in a relationship and claims love "looks on tempests and is never shaken." There are many stormy times within relationships. True love, however, remains strong in the face of troubles and even acts as a guide in getting through them. The speaker asserts, "Love's not Time's fool, though rosy lips and cheeks / Within his bending sickle's compass come," implying that love is not controlled by time. Although people are bound to change in terms of appearance or desirability over time, true love will not be affected. Rather, true love outlasts time to "the edge of doom." In the final lines, the speaker explains that if his claim that "love never changes" is wrong, and if his error is proven to him, then he has never written anything throughout his life. Furthermore, if he is wrong, then no man has ever truly loved. He writes, "If this be error and upon me proved, / I never writ, nor no man ever loved." However, since this poem is proof of his writings, then his view of true love must be correct and man has experienced it.

As a follow-up writing assignment, students choose a Shakespearean sonnet that has not been analyzed in class and write a paragraph stating the generalization about love that the sonnet is making and supporting this claim with evidence and explanations from the text.

An Anthology of First Impressions

After such practice creating an author's generalization, students are ready to work with a longer text. Even so, we have found it useful to have students develop their ideas throughout their reading of the text rather than only at the end. For example, as they complete their reading of Act 1 of *Romeo and Juliet*, students have met all the major characters except Friar Laurence. Shakespeare also has presented quite a few differing views of love, sex, and marriage. As a first step in having students look at characters' views as they may relate to Shakespeare's views of love, we direct them back to the "True Love Opinionnaire" (see Handout 2.18, p. 90) and ask them to review the choices from the perspective of each character listed. Because students have just met these characters, we might ask them only to find one statement with which the character might most agree or disagree. A discussion similar to the one students held regarding their own responses to the "True Love Opinionnaire" then takes place.

To help students further consolidate characters' views of love, sex, and marriage and formulate their first impressions of these characters, we give them the "First Impressions" activity sheet (see Handout 2.23, p. 96) and ask them to add one or more quotations regarding love, sex, or marriage spoken by each character. If students have ready access to the Internet, small groups may collaborate to identify and exchange quotation ideas on a class wiki for homework.

The next step in completing "First Impressions" involves students working in class in small groups of three to five to organize an anthology of their collected Act 1 quotations. In creating their anthologies, all collected quotes must be used and put into one or more groupings, with each grouping sharing a common element. Students then give these quotation groupings titles appropriate to their commonalities. For example, students might decide on headings such as "The Pain of Love" or "Traditional Views of Love and Marriage" or "Looks Equal Love" or "Young Love" or "Extreme Views of Love" or "Marriage Is a Business Deal." Headings will vary among groups, but even groupings such as "Love" and "Marriage" can lead to fruitful discussions. It is most important that students examine the quotations closely in order to identify the characters' initial views of love, marriage, and sex. As student groups work to create their quotation groupings and titles, we circulate among the groups and prompt students to look at specific words and phrases within each quote in order to discover additional meanings.

In addition to the creation of titles here, we often ask students to create titles for scenes or acts of plays or chapters in books. As they do so, students synthesize and evaluate important developments within the work, operating at the complex implied relationship and author's generalization levels of Hillocks's taxonomy. The title format requires that students be succinct, and they enjoy employing their dramatic creativity. Titles in this specific activity allow students to begin their work of generalizations about love, sex, and marriage within the context of the unfolding drama.

After their group work, we ask each group to present one title within their anthology, the quotations it encompasses, and an explanation of how each quotation fits within the title parameters.

By providing students with initial quotes, we model the types of quotations students should be collecting, but we also ask them to search for their own quotes as well so that they review the text after their first reading.

As a follow-up activity for students after they have read Act 2, Scene 3, and met Friar Laurence, we ask them to write a short paragraph in which they identify one of the Friar's quotations referring to love, relate it to one of their Act 1 anthology titles, and explain their thinking. Where do Friar Laurence's sentiments regarding love fall and why? Or does he present a new view? If so, what is it?

Who's Changing? How Do You Know?

After students have completed their first readings of Acts 2 and 3 of *Romeo and Juliet*, it is useful for them to take a second look at their first impressions of some of the main characters with respect to love. Doing so will help students continue to develop their ideas regarding what Shakespeare might be saying about love within the play.

Before asking students to look more closely at the characters of Romeo and Juliet on their own, we lead a whole-class discussion regarding the Nurse. We remind students of the Nurse's quotation related to love and marriage from Act 1, "A man, young lady! Lady, such a man / As all the world—why, he's a man of wax" (1.3.76–77), perhaps directing them to the line or writing it on the board. Then we direct students to the Nurse's lines to Juliet regarding Romeo in 2.5.39–42, "Though his [Romeo's] face be better than any man's, yet his leg excels all men's; and for a hand, and a foot, and a body, though they be not to be talked on, yet, they are past compare." In comparing the Nurse's lines from Acts 1 and 2, students will readily see that the Nurse has not really changed her opinions regarding a good romantic match—physical appearance is still very important to the Nurse. Finally, we ask students to find evidence in Act 3 that either confirms or contradicts the Nurse's previously expressed view of love. Here, students usually will cite the Nurse's reference to

Paris's "fair eye" in Act 3, Scene 5 as she recommends Paris over Romeo to Juliet.

At this point, we direct students to the Act 1 quotations for *Romeo and Juliet* on the "First Impressions" activity sheet as well as any additional quotations for these characters in Act 1 that they found. We then ask students—What about Romeo and Juliet? Have their views of love from Act 1 remained static as the Nurse's have or have they changed from Act 1 to Act 3? What evidence can students provide for their opinions? We ask students to find parallel or contrasting quotations in Acts 2 and 3 to help them answer these questions.

After students have reviewed Acts 2 and 3 for evidence and come to their conclusions regarding Romeo and Juliet, we ask them to pair with another student briefly to compare and explain their ideas. This step allows students to rehearse their explanations, to get feedback from another student, and to consider at least one other perspective before the whole-class discussion.

For the class discussion, students may put their quotation pairs on the board or they may read them aloud, referring their classmates to the appropriate line numbers. A lively discussion usually ensues with some students citing Romeo's "Love is a smoke made with the fume of sighs; / Being purged, a fire sparkling in lovers' eyes; / Being vexed, a sea nourished with lovers' tears. / What is it else? A madness most discreet, / A choking gall, and a preserving sweet" (1.1.190–94) and his "My life were better ended by their hate / Than death prorogued, wanting of thy love" (2.2.77–78) as evidence that Romeo has not changed. He is still a man of extremes when it comes to love. It is all or nothing for him. On the other hand, others may cite Romeo's "Did my heart love till now? Forswear it, sight! / For I ne'er saw true beauty till this night" (1.5.53–54) in Act 1 and his later reference to Juliet as his "soul" in Act 2 ("It is my soul that calls upon my name" (2.2.165)) as evidence that Romeo is no longer just equating beauty with true love but feels a deeper connection with Juliet.

Most students will see a distinct change in Juliet, citing pairs of quotations such as Juliet's first response to her mother's query regarding her thoughts on marriage, "It is an honor that I dream not of" (1.3.67), with any lines in her epithalamium, or wedding speech, beginning 3.2, including "O, I have bought the mansion of a love / But not possessed it, and though I am sold, / Not yet enjoyed. So tedious is this day / As is the night before some festival / To an impatient child that hath new robes / And may not wear them" (3.2.26–31). In comparing Juliet's "I'll look to like if looking liking move, / But no more deep will I endart mine eye / Than your consent gives strength to make it fly" (1.3.98–100) with her later "My bounty is as boundless as the sea, / My love as deep; the more I give to thee, The more I have, for both are infinite" (2.2.133–135), students also might find a change in Juliet's ideas regarding the control and limits of love.

Of course, students also may find parallels between Juliet's "Prodigious birth of love it is to me / That I must love a loathed enemy" (1.55.141–42) and her "'Tis but thy name that is my enemy; / Thou art thyself, though not a Montague" (2.2.38–39). In both they may see that love is not an option for Juliet; she "must" love Romeo and love is stronger than hate. Therefore, she must find a way to reconcile these opposites, as she does in Act 2. Whatever students discover within the text, we follow up with questions asking students to stretch their understanding to the author's generalization level: What might Shakespeare be suggesting about true love? Why might this character have changed? What might this suggest about his or her developing view of love?

If we feel that students need more support at this point, we give students pairs of quotes such as those earlier from Act 1 and Acts 2 and 3 to analyze and draw conclusions rather than having them find their own. However, it is usually better to ask students to review a smaller segment of the text, find their own evidence, and reach their own conclusions if they are ready for this level of independence.

As a follow-up writing activity, students may enjoy writing a "Once/Now" poem in the voice of either Romeo or Juliet. Drawing on the evidence they have found and class discussion, students create a poem with alternating lines beginning with "Once" and "Now." The final poem line is a direct quote from the character within the play. For example, part of a "Once/Now" poem written in the voice of the Nurse might be

> Once I encouraged Juliet to seek a handsome love,
> Now she has found one.
> Once I nursed her as a baby,
> Now Juliet is a wife.
> Once I aided Juliet in her quest to marry Romeo,
> Now I think she should forget him.
> I speak from my heart "And from my soul too. Else beshrew them both."

Teachers may wish to include another following-up writing activity after students read Act 4, Scene 1, which includes the only direct—and perhaps the first?—meeting of Paris and Juliet within the play. At this point we ask students to compare Paris and Juliet's meeting (4.1.17–43) with Romeo and Juliet's first meeting (1.5.94–111). What comparisons and contrasts do they see? What parallel or contrasting evidence can they find? What might these two meetings suggest about Shakespeare's views of true love? Students should use direct evidence from both scenes as well as explanations to support their ideas.

Most Admirable?

Once students have completed their reading of the play, we again ask them to review and consolidate their thinking about the characters and their views of love. To begin discussion, we give students the Most Admirable Ballot (see Handout 2.24, p. 97), go over the instructions with them, and ask them to complete the first column ranking. In asking for this ranking—with no double rankings allowed!—we are asking students to make fine discriminations among the characters and the views of love that they espouse, act upon, and represent.

After students have individually completed their rankings, we begin discussion with a round-robin check-in, in which students in turn orally report their choice for "most admirable" and "least admirable" without further comment. There is never unanimity, and discussion evolves easily from this point, with students wishing to defend their choices and challenge the choices of others with direct evidence from the text (the only defense accepted). In doing so, they are practicing both the skills of argument and close reading of the text. When all ideas have been presented, we ask students to complete the second column of the "Most Admirable Ballot" and to provide evidence for their top two and bottom two choices. As students take this final step, they may find that their rankings are identical to Shakespeare's; however, this step allows them to "respectfully disagree" with the text and yet determine what the author may be saying about love that may differ from their own view. Thus, a student might admire Romeo most as a "man of action" where love is concerned, as someone who embodies "a life without love is not worth living," and yet be able to see that Juliet, the character risking everything to live for love, may be more admirable from Shakespeare's perspective and what the play as a whole suggests.

After these final rankings, we begin discussion by asking students if and how their own rankings differed from those they attributed to Shakespeare. What do they think Shakespeare is saying about true love within this play? About adolescent love? About unconditional love? In a play this rich, there will be several answers.

A Final Writing Assignment

As a final writing assignment assessing students' ability to articulate an author's generalization about a work, we find it is often helpful to identify or have students identify for themselves a genuine "why" question that they would like to explore. In the case of *Romeo and Juliet*, we might offer students the following questions and writing prompt:

- When both characters threaten suicide, why does Friar Laurence scold Romeo but not Juliet?
- Why might Juliet be the last character to die?
- Why does Juliet break with the Nurse at the end of Act 3?
- Why doesn't Romeo wait for confirmation of Juliet's death from Friar Laurence?

Select one of these "why" questions to explore within the context of what Shakespeare is saying about a definition of true love throughout the play. Find, list, and analyze evidence that helps you answer this question. These steps will help you answer your question, create a thesis statement, and identify the significance of what you've found, that is, to formulate a statement regarding what Shakespeare is saying about love.

In exploring answers to genuine questions that they might have about the text, we find students are more invested in their writing. They also are more likely to be focused in their prewriting steps. In addition, they are exploring and articulating how they have come to know something significant about the text—what the author is saying about an important theme or subject within and ultimately beyond the context of the literary work.

Handout 2.18. True Love Opinionnaire

Directions: Read each of the following statements; then write A in the column under "you" if you agree with the statement or D if you disagree with it. No A/D responses allowed!

Characters from *Romeo and Juliet*

Generalizations about love	You	Romeo	Juliet	Nurse	Mer-cutio	Lady Capulet	Lord Capulet	Ben-volio	Paris
1. Physical attraction must precede true love.									
2. People who love each other are best friends.									
3. Love makes you a better person.									
4. You have to work at love.									
5. True love is uncondi-tional.									
6. You should do anything to make the person you love happy.									
7. The spiritual aspects of love are more important than the physical ones.									
8. The course of true love never runs smooth.									
9. If you really love some-one, it's okay to do anything to get him/her to love you back.									
10. People who are in love often do foolish things.									
11. If you truly love some-one, you will not be attracted to anyone else.									
12. You should never give up on love.									
13. Teenagers cannot experience "true" love.									
14. Love at first sight is possible.									
15. If you can't be with the one you love, love the one you're with.									
16. A little love is better than no love.									
17. You are never too young to fall in love.									
18. Love never changes.									
19. Love is blind.									

Handout 2.19. What's Love Got to Do with It?

Directions: Examine the details of the following cartoon; then answer the following questions. Be prepared to present and discuss your answers in a whole-class discussion.

1. What does the term "vet" mean? What service does this street vendor provide?

2. What type of person might be interested in such a service?

3. Identify a statement on the opinionnaire with which the cartoonist might strongly agree or disagree:

What details in the cartoon lead you to your choice?

Writing about Literature, 2nd ed., Revised and Updated by Larry Johannessen, Elizabeth A. Kahn, and Carolyn Calhoun Walter © 2009 NCTE.

Handout 2.20. Analyzing Shakespeare's Sonnet 18

Sonnet 18
by William Shakespeare

Shall I compare thee to a summer's day?
Thou art more lovely and more temperate.
Rough winds do shake the darling buds of May,
And summer's lease hath all too short a date.
Sometimes too hot the eye of heaven shines,
And often is his gold complexion dimmed.
And every fair from fair sometime declines,
By chance or nature's changing course untrimmed.
But thy eternal summer shall not fade,
Nor lose possession of that fair thou owest,
Nor shall Death brag thou wander'st in his shade
When in eternal lines to time thou grow'st.
So long as men can breathe, or eyes can see,
So long lives this, and this gives life to thee.

1. In the comparison made in line 1, who or what is deemed superior? Cite evidence in support of your idea. (Basic Stated Information)

2. Who is "thee" of the sonnet? Whom is the speaker addressing? (Simple Implied Relationship)

3. In what ways is summer personified in the first six lines? (Complex Implied Relationship)

4. Where is "the turn" in the poem? (Simple Implied Relationship)

5. What is "this" (line 14)? (Complex Implied Relationship)

6. How is it possible for "thee" to defeat Death? Cite evidence in support of your idea. (Complex Implied Relationship)

7. What is the speaker saying about love in the first eight lines? What is the speaker suggesting about love in the final six lines? About love and art? (Author's Generalization)

Writing about Literature, 2nd ed., Revised and Updated by Larry Johannessen, Elizabeth A. Kahn, and Carolyn Calhoun Walter © 2009 NCTE.

Handout 2.21. Assessing Shakespeare's Generalizations

Group members: _____, _____, _____,

_____, _____

Directions: Bring copies of Sonnets 18, 29, 61, and 91 for discussion in your small group. Fill in the names of the members of your group. For each of the following sonnets, determine which of the statements listed below most accurately captures what the speaker is saying about love. Base your decision upon specific evidence in the poem, but make sure that your choice captures *the poet's main idea for the entire poem.* Underline your choice and explain your reasoning in writing at the side. If none of the statements seems accurate, create your own.

Sonnet 18

Love and art transcend time.
Through art, love can become eternal.
My true love is better than summer.
Beauty fades but love lasts.
A better option: _____

Sonnet 29

Life brings both love and despair.
Having the love of another can compensate for other deficiencies.
Being in love makes one feel like royalty.
Love is better than money.
A better option: _____

Sonnet 61

True love is jealous.
Unreturned love is a torment.
An unequal love can be disturbing.
Love causes sleeplessness.
A better option: _____

Sonnet 91

Love holds power.
Love creates the greatest happiness, but its absence causes the greatest sorrow.
Love is better than material possessions.
Without love, one cannot be happy.
A better option: _____

Handout 2.22. Explaining a Poet's Generalization

Directions: Imagine that the following sentences are excerpted from a student's written analysis of "Sonnet 116," in which the author's generalization statement is, *The speaker of "Sonnet 116" claims that true love is constant in the face of another's changes, problems, or time.* For each section, select the analysis that you think is most effective in supporting the generalization and, in a sentence or two, explain why. For each of the others that you didn't select, make one or two suggestions for improvement. These may involve issues of content [what is said] or presentation [how ideas are expressed]. Place an asterisk (*) by the letter of the analysis you select. Write all comments below the analyses.

Lines 2–4

(a) In lines 2–4, the speaker declares that love is not genuine when it changes upon finding change.

(b) In lines 2–4, the speaker suggests that "Love is not love / Which alters when it alteration finds, / Or bends with the remover to remove." The speaker is implying that love does not change no matter what else changes.

(c) In lines 2–4, the speaker claims "Love is not love / Which alters when it alteration finds, / Or bends with the remover to remove," implying that true love will remain unchanged even if it discovers its recipient's love alters or changes.

Lines 5 and 6

(a) The speaker also suggests that true love is unshakable, like a lighthouse, "an ever-fixed mark," in the face of problems that arise in a relationship and claims love "looks on tempests and is never shaken." There are many stormy times within relationships. True love, however, remains strong in the face of troubles and even acts as a guide in getting through them.

(b) "It is an ever-fixed mark / That looks on tempests and is never shaken" compares love to a lighthouse that acts as a guide to ships and brings them safely to harbor.

(c) In lines 5 and 6, the speaker is talking about love as "an ever-fixed mark / That looks on tempests and is never shaken." This shows that you should be able to rely on

continued on next page

love to guide you through the tempests or storms that life brings. Problems occur that may involve finances, health, in-laws, etc.

(d) Speaking about true love and how it never changes, the speaker further believes that "It is an ever-fixed mark / That looks on tempests and is never shaken." Again, love never changes.

Lines 9–12
(a) It says in lines 9–12 that "Love's not Time's fool, though rosy lips and cheeks / Within his bending sickle's compass come; / Love alters not with his brief hours and weeks / But bears it out even to the edge of doom," implying that when true love encounters changes, it is not affected. Over time, people are bound to change in terms of appearance or desirability, but true love will not change.

(b) The speaker asserts that "Love's not Time's fool, though rosy lips and cheeks / Within his bending sickle's compass come," implying that love is not controlled by time. Although people are bound to change in terms of appearance or desirability over time, true love will not be affected. Rather, true love outlasts time to "the edge of doom."

Lines 13–14
(a) In the final lines, the speaker gives the clincher to his case: "If this be error and upon me proved, / I never writ, nor no man ever loved." This is showing you that the speaker has to be right. He says if what he has said is wrong and can be proven, then he has never written and no man has ever loved, but he has written this poem, so he has written something and therefore his view of true love must be accurate.

(b) In the final lines, the speaker explains that if his claim that "love never changes" is wrong, and if his error is proven to him, then he has never written anything throughout his life. Furthermore, if he is wrong, then no man has ever truly loved. He writes, "If this be error and upon me proved, / I never writ, nor no man ever loved." However, since this poem is proof of his writings, then his view of true love must be correct and man has experienced it.

Writing about Literature, 2nd ed., Revised and Updated by Larry Johannessen, Elizabeth A. Kahn, and Carolyn Calhoun Walter © 2009 NCTE.

Handout 2.23. First Impressions: Act 1 of *Romeo and Juliet*

Directions: Add one or more quotations regarding love, sex, or marriage for each character listed. Working with others, review your collection of quotes in order to create an anthology entitled "Sentiments Regarding Love and Marriage." Follow these guidelines:

- Create divisions or categories for your anthology by looking for common views among your collected materials and grouping these quotations together.
- Give each grouping a title that reflects the commonality you've discovered.
- A quotation may be included in more than one grouping if appropriate, and all quotations need to be included in at least one grouping.

Character	Quotation	Additional Quotations
Romeo	"Love is a smoke made with the fume of sighs; / Being purged, a fire sparkling in lovers' eyes; / Being vexed, a sea nourished with lovers' tears. / What is it else? A madness most discreet, / A choking gall, and a preserving sweet" (1.1.190–4).	
Benvolio	"Tut, man, one fire burns out another's burning / One pain is lessened by another's anguish" (1.2.45–6).	
Paris	"But now, my lord, what say you to my suit?" (1.2.6).	
Lord Capulet	"But woo her, gentle Paris, get her heart; / My will to her consent is but a part" (1.2.16–7)	
Lady Capulet	"Well, think of marriage now. Younger than you / Here in Verona, ladies of esteem / Are made already mothers" (1.3.70–2).	
Nurse	"A man, young lady! Lady, such a man / As all the world—Why, he's a man of wax" (1.3.76–7).	
Juliet	"I'll look to like if looking liking move, / But no more deep will I endart mine eye / Than your consent gives strength to make it fly" (1.3.98–100).	
Mercutio	"If love be rough with you, be rough with love" (1.4.27).	

List anthology titles and the line numbers of quotations covered by them:

Handout 2.24. Most Admirable?

Directions: 1. Taking into account both a character's words and actions, whom do you consider most admirable with respect to love? Rank each of the characters listed below from most admirable (1) to least admirable (9) with respect to their views of love and marriage—no double choices allowed!—in the column marked "Your Ranking." Be prepared to offer reasons and evidence from the text in support of your choices.

2. Taking into account both a character's words and actions, whom would Shakespeare consider most admirable with respect to love? Rank each of the characters listed below from most admirable (1) to least admirable (9) with respect to their views of love and marriage as you believe Shakespeare would in the column marked "Shakespeare." Cite line numbers of evidence from the text in support of your top two and bottom two choices.

Character	Your Ranking	Shakespeare's Ranking
Lord Capulet		
Paris		
Lady Capulet		
Nurse		
Juliet		
‍ieo		
‍lio		
‍tio		
‍urence		

Writing about Literature, 2nd ed., Revised and Updated by Larry Johannessen, Elizabeth A. Kahn, and Carolyn Calhoun Walter © 2009 NCTE.

References

Alexander, P. A., Jetton, T. L., Kulikowich, J. M., & Woehler, C. A. (1994). Contrasting instructional and structural importance: The seductive effect of teacher questions. *Journal of Reading Behavior, 26*(1), 19–45.

Applebee, A., Langer, J. A., Nystrand, M., & Gamoran, A. (2003). Discussion-based approaches to developing understanding: Classroom instruction and student performance in middle and high school English. *American Educational Research Journal, 40*(3), 685–730.

Barnet, S. (1972). *The complete signet classic Shakespeare.* New York: Harcourt Brace Jovanovich.

Beaufort, A. (1998). Transferring writing knowledge to the workplace: Are we on track? In M. S. Garay, & S. A. Bernhardt (Eds.), *Expanding literacies: English teaching and the new workplace* (pp. 179–199). Albany: State University of New York Press.

Beaufort, A. (2006). Writing in the professions. In P. Smagorinsky (Ed.), *Research on composition: Multiple perspectives on two decades of change* (pp. 217–242). New York: Teachers College Press.

Beaufort, A. (1999). *Writing in the real world: Making the transition from school to work.* New York: Teachers College Press.

Beers, K., & Odell, L. (2005). *Holt elements of literature. Third course.* Austin, TX: Holt, Rinehart, and Winston.

Beers, K., & Odell, L. (2005). *Holt elements of literature. Fifth course.* Austin, TX: Holt, Rinehart, and Winston.

Bloom, B. S. (1956). *Taxonomy of educational objectives: The classification of education goals.* New York: McKay.

Bruner, J. S. (1962). Introduction. In L. S. Vygotsky, *Thought and language* (pp. v–x). Cambridge, MA: MIT Press.

Christenbury, L., & Kelly, P. P. (1983). *Questioning: A path to critical thinking.* Urbana, IL: ERIC/NCTE.

Cisneros, S. (1989). *The house on Mango Street.* New York: Vintage Books.

Connor, U. (1990). Linguistic/rhetorical measures for international persuasive student writing. *Research in the Teaching of English, 24*(1), 67–87.

Daniels, H. (2005). *An introduction to Vygotsky* (2nd ed.). New York: Routledge.

Dias, P., Freedman, A., Medway, P., & Paré, A. (1999). *Worlds apart: Acting and writing in academic and workplace contexts.* Mahwah, NJ: L. Erlbaum Associates.

Fisher, D. (2006). *Improving adolescent literacy: Strategies at work.* Keynote presentation at Illinois Association of Teachers of English Conference, Peoria, IL, October 13–14.

Fisher, D., & Frey, N. (2004). *Improving adolescent literacy: Strategies at work.* Upper Saddle River, NJ: Pearson/Merrill/Prentice Hall.

Flower, L. S., & Hayes, J. R. (1977). Problem-solving strategies and the writing process. *College English, 39*(4), 449–461.

Graff, G. (2003). *Clueless in academe: How schooling obscures the life of the mind.* New Haven, CT: Yale University Press.

Hedegaard, M. (2005). The zone of proximal development as a basis for instruction. In H. Daniels (Ed.), *An introduction to Vygotsky* (2nd ed., pp. 227–251). New York: Routledge.

Hillocks, G., Jr. (2006). Middle and high school composition. In P. Smagorinsky (Ed.), *Research on composition: Multiple perspectives on two decades of change* (pp. 48–77). New York: Teachers College Press.

Hillocks, G., Jr. (1986). *Research on written composition: New directions for teaching.* New York: National Conference on Research in English; and Urbana, IL: ERIC Clearinghouse on Reading and Communication Skills, National Institute of Education.

Hillocks, G., Jr. (2002). *The testing trap: How state writing assessments control learning.* New York: Teachers College Press.

Hillocks, G., Jr. (1980). Toward a hierarchy of skills in the comprehension of literature. *English Journal, 69*(3), 54–59.

Hillocks, G., Jr., & Ludlow, L. H. (1984). A taxonomy of skills in reading and interpreting fiction. *American Educational Research Journal, 21*(1),7–27.

Hillocks, G., Jr., McCabe, B. J., & McCampbell, J. F. (1971). *The dynamics of English instruction, grades 7–12.* New York: Random House.

Insanity defense. *'Lectric Law Library.* Retrieved December 31, 2006, from http://www.lectlaw.com/def/d029.htm.

Johannessen, L. (1993). Digging into *Julius Caesar* through character analysis. In J. E. Davis, & R. E. Salomone (Eds.), *Teaching Shakespeare today: Practical approaches and productive strategies* (pp. 207–217). Urbana, IL: National Council of Teachers of English.

Johannessen, L. (2001). Enhancing response to literature through character analysis. *The Clearing House, 74*(3), 145–50.

Johannessen, L., Kahn, E., and Walter, C. (1982). *Designing and sequencing prewriting activities.* Urbana, IL: ERIC/NCTE.

Lee, H. (1960). *To kill a mockingbird.* New York: Warner Books.

Langer, J. A. (2001). Beating the odds: Teaching middle and high school students to read and write well. *American Educational Research Journal, 38*(4), 837–80.

Light, R. (2001). *Making the most of college.* Cambridge, MA: Harvard University Press.

McCann, T. M. (1989). Student argumentative writing knowledge and ability at three grade levels. *Research in the Teaching of English, 23*(1), 62–76.

McCann, T. M., Johannessen, L. R., Kahn, E., & Flanagan, J. M. (2006). *Talking in class: Using discussion to enhance teaching and learning.* Urbana, IL: NCTE.

National Center for Education Statistics. (2005). *NAEP 2004 trends in academic progress: Three decades of student performance in reading and mathematics: Findings in brief* (NCES Publication No. 2005-463). U. S. Department of Education, Institute of Education Sciences, National Center for Education Statistics. Washington, D. C.: U. S. Government Printing Office.

National Commission on Writing in America's Schools and Colleges. (2003). *The neglected "R": The need for a writing revolution.* New York: The College Entrance Examination Board.

Nystrand, M. (2006). Research on the role of classroom discourse as it affects reading comprehension. *Research in the Teaching of English, 40*(4), 392–412.

Pearson, P. D., & Johnson, D. D. (1978). *Teaching reading comprehension.* New York: Holt, Rinehart, and Winston.

Prentice Hall literature (Grade 9): Timeless voices, timeless themes. Gold. (2000). Upper Saddle River, NJ: Prentice Hall Inc.

Rosenblatt, L. M. (1968). *Literature as exploration* (3rd ed.). New York: Noble and Noble.

Santa, C. M., Havens, L. T., & Valdes, B. J. (2004). *Project CRISS: Creating independence through student-owned strategies* (3rd ed.). Dubuque, Iowa: Kendall/Hunt.

Sellen, A. J., & Harper, R. (2002). *The myth of the paperless office.* Cambridge, MA: MIT Press.

Shakespeare, W., & Bevington, D. (1988). *Romeo and Juliet.* New York: Bantam Books.

Shaughnessy, M. P. (1977). *Errors and expectations: A guide for the teacher of basic writing.* New York: Oxford University Press.

Smagorinsky, P., & Fry, P. K. (1993). The social environment of the classroom: A Vygotskian perspective on small group process. *Communication Education, 42*(2), 159–171.

Smagorinsky, P., & Smith, M. W. (1992). The nature of knowledge in composition and literary understanding: The question of specificity. *Review of Educational Research, 62*(3), 279–305.

Smith, M. W. (1991). *Understanding unreliable narrators: Reading between the lines in the literature classroom.* Theory & Research into Practice. Urbana, IL: NCTE.

Smith, M. W., & Hillocks, G., Jr. (1988). Sensible sequencing: Developing knowledge about literature text by text. *English Journal, 77*(6), 44–49.

Smith, M. W., & Wilhelm, J. D. (2006). *Going with the flow: How to engage boys (and girls) in their literacy learning.* Portsmouth, N.H.: Heinemann.

Squire, J. R. (1983). Composing and comprehending: Two sides of the same basic process. *Language Arts, 60*(5), 581–589.

Steinbeck, J. *The pearl.* (1974). New York: Bantam Books.

Toulmin, S. E. (1958). *The uses of argument.* Cambridge, UK: Cambridge University Press.

Toulmin, S. E., Rieke, R. D., & Janik, A. (1984). *An introduction to reasoning* (2nd ed.). New York: Macmillan.

Troyka, L. Q. (1973). *A study of the effects of simulation-gaming on expository prose competence of remedial English composition students.* Unpublished doctoral dissertation, New York University.

Twain, M., & Cohen, R. (1965). *The adventures of Huckleberry Finn.* New York: Bantam Books.

Vygotsky, L. S., & Cole, M. (1978). *Mind in society: The development of higher psychological processes.* Cambridge, MA: Harvard University Press.

Walker, Alice. (2007). Everyday use. In *Prentice Hall literature: The American experience* (pp. 1090–1098). Upper Saddle River, NJ: Pearson Education, Inc.

Wells, G. (2000). Dialogic inquiry in education: Building on the legacy of Vygotsky. In C. D. Lee & P. Smagorinsky (Eds.), *Vygotskian perspectives on literacy research: Building on the legacy of Vygotsky* (pp. 51–85). Cambridge, UK: Cambridge University Press.

Wiggins, G. P., & McTighe, J. (1998). *Understanding by design.* Alexandria, VA: Association for Supervision and Curriculum Development.

Wright, B. D., & Masters, G. N. (1982). *Rating scale analysis.* Chicago: MESA Press.

Wright, B. D., Masters, G. N., & Ludlow, L. (1981). *CREDIT.* Chicago: MESA Psychometric Laboratory, University of Chicago.

Writing Study Group of the NCTE Executive Committee. (2004). *NCTE beliefs about the teaching of writing.* Urbana, IL: NCTE.

Yeh, S. S. (1998). Empowering education: Teaching argumentative writing to cultural minority middle-school students. *Research in the Teaching of English, 33*(1), 49–83.

Authors

Larry R. Johannessen is a professor in the Department of English at Northern Illinois University, where he teaches in the English education program and literature courses primarily dealing with the Vietnam War. He holds a B.A. from California State University East Bay, Hayward, California, and an M.A.T. and Ph.D. from the University of Chicago. He taught high school English and history for 10 years. In addition to chapters in books, he has contributed more than 70 articles to scholarly journals, including *Research in the Teaching of English, English Journal, Journal of Adolescent & Adult Literacy, Educational Leadership, The Clearing House, The Social Studies, Illinois English Bulletin, Virginia English Bulletin, North Carolina English Teacher, Arizona English Bulletin, The Wisconsin English Journal,* and *Classroom Notes Plus.* With Thomas M. McCann, he is the coauthor of *In Case You Teach English: An Interactive Casebook for Prospective and Practicing Teachers* (Merrill/ Prentice Hall, 2002). He coauthored *Talking in Class: Using Discussion to Enhance Teaching and Learning* (NCTE, 2006). He is a coeditor of *Reflective Teaching, Reflective Learning* (Heinemann, 2005). He is author of *Illumination Rounds: Teaching the Literature of the Vietnam War* (NCTE, 1992) and coauthor of two popular NCTE publications: *Writing about Literature* (NCTE, 1984) and *Designing* and *Sequencing Prewriting Activities* (NCTE, 1982). He is listed in *Who's Who Among America's Teachers* and *Who's Who in American Education.* He has collaborated with Thomas M. McCann and Bernard Ricca on research about the concerns of teachers during their formative years of teaching (*Supporting Beginning English Teachers*: NCTE, 2005). For this work, McCann, Johannessen, and Ricca earned NCTE's 2006 Richard A. Meade Award for Research in English Education. He lives in Wheaton, Illinois, with his wife, Elizabeth.

Elizabeth A. Kahn has taught English language arts for 31 years, currently at James B. Conant High School, where she serves as chair of the English department. She earned a B.A. in English from Wake Forest University, and a M.A.T. in English and a Ph.D. in curriculum and instruction from the University of Chicago. She is a coeditor of *Reflective Teaching, Reflective Learning* (Heinemann, 2005), and coauthor of *Talking in Class: Using Discussion to Enhance Teaching and Learning* (NCTE, 2006), *Writing about Literature* (NCTE, 1984), and *Designing and Sequencing Prewriting Activities* (NCTE, 1982). She has published articles in *Research in the Teaching of English, English Journal, Journal of Educational Research, Clearing House, Curriculum Review,* and *Illinois English Bulletin.* She recently served on the NCTE Secondary Section Steering Committee and is a National Board Certified Teacher. Ms. Kahn lives in Wheaton, Illinois, with her husband Larry Johannessen.

Carolyn Calhoun Walter has taught English language arts in both public and private school settings, and currently at The University of Chicago Laboratory Schools. She has served as department head and taught high school students of all levels and abilities. In addition to her teaching, she has worked as a freelance writer and editor for several publishing companies. She earned a B.A. in English from The College of Wooster and a M.A.T. in English from The University of Chicago. She has made professional presentations at local, state, and national levels and is the coauthor of *Writing about Literature* (NCTE, 1984) and *Designing and Sequencing Prewriting Activities* (NCTE, 1982) as well as articles appearing in *Clearing House, English Journal,* and *Curriculum Review.* Ms. Walter lives in Oak Park, Illinois, with her husband James. They have two grown children, Jay and Claire. After graduating from college in 2007, Claire became a fourth-generation English teacher, having made a two-year commitment to Teach for America in Baltimore, Maryland.

This book was typeset in Palatino and Helvetica by Electronic Imaging.
Typefaces used on the cover were Adobe Garamond and Optima.
The book was printed on 50-lb. Williamsburg Offset paper by Versa Press, Inc.